Jesse!
You are loved
Jesus! Rejoice,

Jonathan Wilbur

John 4:14

MW01295980

The Women Jesus Loved

The Women Jesus Loved drew on my heart strings like no other. I was drawn into each woman's struggle, desperation, and plight that in many ways is still being fought today. Each story was told with such detail and emotion, a story of the faith of women and how their faith moved Jesus, the real Jesus, the one who loved and still loves and cherishes women. Jesus' compassion for women is just as stunning today as it was 2000 years ago! Thank you, Jonathan, for sharing this truth with us!

– Judi Noble
Executive Director-Eagle's Wings
www.eagleswingsglobal.org

It is an honor to recommend *The Women Jesus Loved* to all readers, men and women alike. The scriptures come alive as Jonathan Williams enhances stories of women with well researched historical and cultural facts. You will find yourself understanding and relating to characters that lived 2000 years ago like never before. The reflection questions at the end of each story challenged me to open my heart more deeply to a loving God. This book allowed me to see that Jesus Christ began a radical movement of loving women well and awakening their hearts with grace. I've realized that believers, including myself, need to continue this movement in order to set women throughout the world free to see many aspects of God come to life.

– Susan Milligan
Co-founder of Lock & Key Ministries
co-author of *Moving Him In: 12 Tangible Keys
to Preparing a Place for Christ*

Jonathan brings familiar biblical stories to life, capturing Jesus' deep love, compassion, and respect for the hurting women he encountered. Jesus' actions contrasted sharply with the culture and leaders of the day who openly condemned, judged, and disregarded them. I highly recommend this book! It gives you insight into the heart of Jesus and a vital recognition of the dignity and elevation Jesus offered to women.

– Karla Downing, M.A., MFT
Licensed Marriage and Family Therapist
Author of *10 Lifesaving Principles for Women in Difficult Marriages* and Founder of ChangeMyRelationship.com

I love how this book is written! Time and attention to historical and cultural details creates rich stories of the Bible stories we know so well. Each chapter gives you a chance to explore more deeply what God reveals to us through the questions and reflections. Williams identifies with the women and his words are written with compassion and thoughtfulness as though he walked in their shoes.

– Shea Wood
Co-founder of Lock & Key Ministries
co-author of *Moving Him In: 12 Tangible Keys to Preparing a Place for Christ*

The Women Jesus Loved

Jonathan Williams

ISBN-13: 978-1494964016
ISBN-10: 1494964015

DEDICATION

I have been blessed with the love of many women — my mother, my sisters, my first wife now with the Lord, my wife who is my best friend, my daughter, my daughters-in-law, my nieces, and the countless friends and other family members who have shown me the love of Christ. They have loved Jesus deeply and been among the women loved by him.

I dedicate this book to all of you. May it bless you and multitudes of others by drawing you close to the One who loves you the most.

CONTENTS

Jesus and Women

A trendy discussion, and belief for some people is that Jesus loved and married Mary Magdalene. This has been unfortunate for two reasons.

First, there is no historical evidence for such a marriage.[1] Second, it obscures something far more important and radical – the attitude and actions of Jesus toward women. In a world filled with men who have treated and continue to treat women as second-class citizens at best and as objects of pleasure or property at worst, Jesus stands apart. *Jesus loved women* with the liberating love of God.

The Women Jesus Loved is an imaginative, Scripturally faithful exploration of familiar stories in the New Testament where Jesus interacted with women. The fact that he interacted with them at all was astonishing in his time, but the way in which he spoke with them, the mercy he gave, and the importance he bestowed upon them revealed a message the world needed to hear and still needs to hear– God loves women as much as he loves men, and women are equally valuable in his eyes and must be treated with equal respect and honor.

For those familiar with the stories of Jesus, this will not come as a surprise and hardly seem revolutionary. But if we could time-travel back to the ancient world or even transport ourselves to some parts of our world, we would find Jesus' attitude toward women a bold departure from many cultural and religious norms.

---

[1] For example, the most recent "spectacular finding" of an ancient reference to Jesus' wife proved to be a modern forgery.

In Jesus' day, only men were considered disciples, or learners. Jesus had women disciples.[2] The third century BC writings of *Ben Sirach* warned against women supporting men financially. Jesus and his twelve apostles were supported by the generous donations of women.[3] When Jesus told stories illustrating important truths about the kingdom of God, women were just as likely to be the heroes in the stories as men.[4] Jesus traveled from village to village preaching and teaching and women were in his entourage. Undoubtedly, he took great care to protect their reputation and to provide for their safety, but it was unheard of for women to spend the night in strange villages if they were not with relatives.

Why is all of this important? That may be a question only you can answer. I do know one answer that is urgent for the time in which we live. Women are suffering throughout the world simply because they are women. Untold millions are treated as second class citizens at best and, heartbreakingly, slaves or property at worst. Did you know that:

- 200,000 Nepali women and girls have been kidnapped or sold by destitute parents into India's brothels and 12-14,000 more are trafficked each year?

- 50,000 little girls are domestic servants in Morocco and some of them are made to work 16 hours a day, sleep on the floor, and eat only scraps?

- Battering is the single largest cause of injury to women

---

[2] In Matthew 12:48-50 women were among his disciples, and the story of Luke 10:38-42 says that Mary "sat at his feet," a technical phrase for a disciple.
[3] See Luke 8:1-3.
[4] See Kenneth Bailey, *Jesus Through Middle Eastern Eyes*, IVP, 194-195.

between the ages of 15-44 in the United States?

- In the U.K. two women a week are killed by current or former partners?

- In Mexico, 21 out of 32 states do not consider it a crime for a man to beat his wife?

- Women in Swaziland are expected to remain silent when abused and the Swati word for "wife" or "woman" means "one who dies without speaking of what she has endured"?

- 2/3 of the world's 880 million illiterates are women?

- In some places in China, daughters have been called "maggots in the rice" because they take food that could go to boys and 50 million women have gone "missing" because of institutionalized killing and neglect?[5]

This depressing list could go on for pages.

It is time for the world to take a new look at women through the eyes of Jesus. *The Women Jesus Loved* is one such look. The stories in this book are taken from my larger list of stories that I call *Stories of the Master*, my retelling of the story of Jesus and the stories he told using historical and cultural details that we modern people often miss, but details which make the stories come alive. You can listen to this growing list of stories at www.WGSministries.org/Stories.

I am indebted to the works of many scholars that I have read

---

[5] These statistics taken from *True Grit: Women Taking on the World for God's Sake*, by Deborah Meroff, published by georgeverwer.com

through the years who have given me new eyes as I read the Gospels. I note two in particular.

Dr. Kenneth Bailey spent 40 years living and teaching New Testament in Egypt, Lebanon, Jerusalem, and Cyprus. He is the emeritus research professor of Middle Eastern New Testament studies for the Tantur Ecumenical Institute in Jerusalem and is the author of many enlightening works including *Jesus Through Middle Eastern Eyes*. Dr. Gary Burge is professor of New Testament at Wheaton College and the author of numerous books including *Jesus: The Middle Eastern Storyteller*. You will find that I reference them throughout the book.

One of my listeners, a young man who lives in a country closed to the Gospel asked, "Jonathan, where do you get all of your information? The stories you present are so much fuller than in the Gospels." My answer is twofold: I have learned many details from the men I have mentioned and from others, and I weave these details into the stories. I also have had to create minor events and conversations between Jesus and the people to whom he spoke to "fill in the gaps" of the brief biblical accounts. This is part of "story crafting" and my hope and prayer is that I have remained faithful to the spirit of the original story and to the truth of who Jesus is and why he came as presented in the biblical accounts.

Finally, each story is presented in four parts.

- The Story
- The Story as originally told in the Gospels
- Cultural and Historical Insights
- Reflection to make the story personal for you and for others with whom you learn.

My prayer for all who read this book is that they would see Jesus with fresh eyes and come to experience his saving love just as the women in these stories did.

My prayer also is that God would use this book to liberate women – and men – from the suffering and slaveries that still exist in the world today.

The kingdom of God and of his Messiah draws near!

Jonathan Williams

Jonathan Williams

The Woman Who Wept at His Feet

She stood at the edge of the crowd not daring to come closer because of her shame. She desperately wanted to talk with Jesus, but how, and if she did what would she say? More importantly, what would he say to her for the way she had lived?

Jonathan Williams

1 THE WOMAN WHO WEPT AT HIS FEET

She stood at the edge of the crowd. She had heard about Jesus, his miracles and his teaching, and she desperately wanted to see and hear him. She had so much she needed to say, so much to tell about her life, and so many questions to ask, but what chance did she have of ever getting close enough to talk with him and have him speak personally to her? Besides, she was a sinner. She had a reputation in her community and she must be discreet when in public so as not to arouse hostility from others.

She listened as Jesus spoke and even though the distance was almost too great to hear, it was as if Jesus was speaking directly to her. As he spoke all her sins came up before her eyes, all her unworthiness, all her shame, and she began to cry. It had been a long time since she cried. Her heart had been hardened by the bad choices she had made in life and by the mistreatment from men and the anger of the other women in the community. It is as if her heart had been baked by the hot middle eastern sun and it was dry and unfeeling.

Yet when Jesus spoke of God's kingdom coming with love,

forgiveness, mercy, healing, and restoration, she felt a stirring inside. His words washed over her, softening her and penetrating deep into the soil of her heart, enlivening it, nourishing it, and giving her hope. She began to cry again, but this time the tears were different because she felt different. She was feeling again. Her heart was coming alive. She sensed the love of God, the mercy of God for someone such as she was, and it was all because of this man Jesus and the words he spoke that day.

The message was over and Jesus, surrounded by a group of men, began to walk her way. She stood still, watching, and pulled her shawl more closely across her face and body so others would not identify her. How she longed to be close to Jesus and talk to him! They were now right next to her and she heard Simon the Pharisee say, "Jesus, what you have stated today is a hard word to receive. I would like to discuss this more with you. Several experts in the Law are coming to my house today to discuss Moses and the Prophets. I would like you to come also and join us for lunch so that we can discuss these matters further."

Jesus replied, "I accept your invitation Simon," and with that, the men continued walking toward the house of Simon the Pharisee. The woman could not believe her good fortune. She knew where Jesus would be next – at the home of Simon the Pharisee, and if she hurried, she could be there at his house for the lunch. She would not be an invited guest. Only the men would recline at the table, but villagers were allowed to come into the home and stand to the side of the feasting men, watching, listening, and learning as the invited guests discussed matters of great spiritual importance.

The crowd would be great in the house and there would not be room for all. She had only a moment to decide, and then the woman hurried to her home to get something of great value. She then hurried toward the house of Simon the Pharisee, hoping against hope that she would get there before Jesus, Simon, and the experts on the Law and that she would be allowed to enter.

Breathlessly she came to the street where Simon lived and in the distance she saw him and the others with Jesus. Good, she was ahead of them, and she walked quickly and discreetly to his home and slipped in unnoticed.

Servants were scurrying with last minute preparations for the meal. Several other villagers were entering the house and the room where the meal would be served. Many men and women like herself had come to watch the meal and hear the conversation between Jesus and Simon the Pharisee. Soon the men would be deep in discussion over Jesus' message.

She was relieved when no one recognized her or asked what she was doing there. There was such noise and busyness going on, and she was able to find a place that gave her full view of the door through which Jesus would walk and the place where he and the others would recline at table and talk.

Her heart was pounding within her and she clutched the small bottle at her breast that held her precious perfume. If only she could give this to Jesus as a gift. It is the least she could do for all he had done for her. She had not even met him and yet she felt so close to him and felt such love and release that she had not felt in years.

"They are here! They are here!" one of the servants excitedly exclaimed, and the men walked through the room. First was Simon, the master of the house and then his friends. As each one entered they were given a kiss and their feet washed. Some were anointed with oil and great honor was bestowed, one by one, to each Pharisee who entered. The woman watched the entire proceeding with fascination as each man was honored, and she thought of her great desire to bring honor to Jesus and wondered how Simon would honor him.

Then, something odd caught her attention. She saw Simon talking with the servants and she heard snatches of his orders to them, "When he enters the room … do not …" and then the voices were muffled. Then she heard, "… no water for his feet …" and "… no oil…." Why was Simon saying this? What was he referring to?

Finally, Jesus entered the house and into the banqueting hall. He took two steps in and stopped. At this point servants were to come forward with water for his feet and Simon was to come forward in gracious hospitality with a kiss on the hands or the cheeks. But no one moved. The servants stood helplessly. They looked to Simon but his stone face warned them that they were not to make a move in the direction of Jesus. And there Jesus stood, alone, shamed, and dishonored in the house of Simon the Pharisee. Had not Simon invited him? Was he not his guest? Then why was he not given the marks of hospitality? Why was there no kiss for Jesus as the others had received? Why was there no water for his feet? Why was there no oil for his head?

Jesus had walked into a trap. He looked at Simon who smiled at him, not a smile of friendship but a smile of one who has conquered an enemy. He looked at the other Pharisees who were already reclining at table but who refused to make eye contact with him. He looked at the servants and smiled at them as if he were saying, "It's OK. I understand." Then, Jesus walked to his place at the table and reclined.

The guests who had watched this oversight, this insult could not believe what they had just witnessed. Jesus was forced to eat with unwashed hands. He would be ceremonially unclean, yet he went forward to the meal anyway. Jesus had just been publicly insulted by one of the leading men of the village, yet he stayed and took his place at the meal with great dignity and composure.

The guests were surprised by what they had just seen. The room was now charged with anxiety as people held their breath wondering what would happen next, and the woman stood in shock as she saw the humiliating treatment Jesus had endured by these men who claimed to be the representatives of God. She looked to the servants and pleaded with her eyes for them to do something for Jesus, but they could only look back with weak, helpless smiles. She looked around at the table of dignitaries. Not one of them had fulfilled the rules of hospitality. All of them had insulted Jesus.

She wanted to go to each of them, shake them, slap them, scream at them for the way they had treated this man who now meant so much to her, this man who had given her hope, this man who had given her a new life.

Her heart pounded within her and she knew what she must do. "Very well," she said to herself, and she walked to the men who were beginning their lunch and stood silently behind the feet of Jesus. She was supposed to stay by the back wall with all the other villagers who were there to watch the meal and listen to the conversation. She felt like all eyes were upon her and that many were thinking, "Who is this woman and why is she not taking her proper place?"

The woman took a deep breath. She thought on all that Jesus had said, she thought on what he had come to mean to her, and then she whispered, "if no one else will do this, I will." She knelt beside his feet and looked at the servants for water. She dare not speak aloud where men were gathered to discuss important matters but everyone knew what she wanted. She wanted water to wash Jesus' feet. If no one else would do it. If no servant of Simon the Pharisee would do it, then she would wash his feet! But no one moved, and the woman looked in grief and anger at their hardness of heart.

Her tears came in ever greater torrents and she could now wash the feet of Jesus. Her sorrow had provided the water she needed to perform the act of honor and respect.

And then she burst into tears, tears for what they were doing to her master, tears for the way they had insulted the only man who had ever loved her and respected her, tears for her own sin, and tears for the mercy she had received. And as she knelt at his feet, sobbing with great sorrow over all the emotions roiling through her heart, her tears began to fall upon his feet and wet them. At last, there was water for his feet. And then the tears came in ever greater torrents as she realized what was happening and that now she could wash the feet of Jesus. Her sorrow had provided the water she needed to perform the act of honor and respect, and with great gentleness she moved her hands across his feet and washed the dust away.

But now she had to dry his feet. She looked up at everyone, at the Pharisees, at the ones standing besides the wall, at the servants. She needed a towel to dry Jesus' feet. But still no one moved. "Very well," she thought. "I have come this far. I have come into the home of a Pharisee. I have walked to a place in the room where I am not supposed to be. I have let my tears fall upon the feet of this holy man Jesus and washed them with my sinful hands. I will not stop now."

And the woman did the unthinkable. She did what no one in that part of the world did in public. She let down her hair in the sight of all. Only a wife at home in the presence of her husband did such a thing. Slowly, knowing that every eye was upon her, she let down her long, beautiful hair, brought it in front of her body and stooped even lower and began to dry his feet with her hair.

The act was exhilarating! She did not care what others thought. In the past she had used her body for sin, and now she was using her body to worship and bring honor! The woman was overwhelmed with joy at this new experience of pure love, and she began kissing his feet – in humility, in gratitude, and in worship for God's mercy in her life. Again and again she kissed his feet. Then the woman raised up slightly and put her hand in her bosom and brought out her most precious possession, perfumed oil. She would not presume to touch Jesus' hands or his head. She stayed at his feet and anointed them with the oil.

The servants who watched the woman were ashamed for their lack of courage as the woman did what they should have done. The guests who were in the room were wondering what would happen next to this sinful woman who had dared to approach Jesus in the home of Simon the Pharisee. But the Pharisees who watched these events unfold in front of them recoiled in horror and revulsion as if some plague had entered the house and was threatening them. They could not believe the boldness of this sinful woman and her complete lack of modesty. But their greatest shock was that Jesus himself did nothing to the woman. He did not move. He did not protest. He did not ask the servants to remove her from the house. In fact, he seemed to be enjoying what the woman was doing.

Simon the Pharisee, with a knowing look on his face mumbled to the Pharisee next to him, "If this man were a prophet he would know who this woman is and what kind of person she is and would not allow her to touch him. He would know what a terrible sinner she is."

But Jesus turned to Simon and said, "Simon, I have something to say to you."

And Simon the Pharisee said, "Say it, teacher."

And Jesus said, "A moneylender had two men in debt to him. One man owed him 500 silver coins. The other one owed him 50 silver coins. Both were unable to pay their debts, and the moneylender graciously forgave them both. Which of the two will love him more?"

The tables were now turned. Simon had invited Jesus to his house for lunch but his goal was to put him in his place by insulting him when he walked through his doors by not offering him water for washing, a kiss for the cheek, or oil for his head. He had set a trap for Jesus, but his trap was undone by the unexpected actions of a woman and by a parable that revealed the truth for all to see and hear. To save face, Simon answered, "I ... suppose the one whom he forgave more."

"I suppose?" Didn't he know? Of course he knew. Everyone knew the answer to Jesus' simple question from his simple story, but he had a hard time admitting the truth even though it was looking at him right in the face through the eyes of a lowly, sinful woman who provided water, a towel, kisses, and anointing oil that he, as the master of the house, had failed to provide.

Jesus turned to the woman who continued to kiss his feet in

worship and anoint them with her costly perfume and said to Simon, "Do you see this woman? I entered your house. You gave me no water for my feet but she has wet my feet with her tears and wiped them with her hair. You gave me no kiss. But she, since the time I came in has not ceased to kiss my feet. You did not anoint my head with oil, but she anointed my feet with perfume."

"For this reason, I say to you Simon, that her sins, which are many have been forgiven for she loved much. But he who is forgiven little, loves little."

Jesus then reached down and touched her shoulders. With one hand he lifted her face and looked deep into her eyes and said to her, "Your sins have been forgiven."

The Pharisees could not believe what they had just heard. As if it were not enough that Jesus would let such a woman touch him, now he was claiming to forgive her sins. Who did he think he was? But while they were choking on their lunch over what the woman did and what Jesus said, Jesus said to the woman, "Your faith has saved you, go in peace."

The sinful woman stood up, took one more look at Jesus, and walked out the door with her head held high, deep peace in her heart, and her life washed clean. Her desires were fulfilled beyond her wildest imaginations. When she had heard Jesus teach earlier in the day her heart had been touched by the love of God and she felt her soul coming alive again as the forgiveness and mercy of God spread through her. She had longed to be close to Jesus and to thank him but she had no idea how she could get close to him.

But at the home of Simon the Pharisee, God opened a door for her to worship Jesus and honor him.

~~~

The Woman Who Wept at His Feet – this story has been told countless times through the ages, and now it has been told to you. I would like to ask you this question. "Who in the story are you most like?" Several kinds of people make themselves known in the story.

First, are the Pharisees, self confident, self assured, self righteous, and self absorbed. They thought they had a corner on the truth. They thought they had everything figured out. And they thought they knew better than Jesus. Simon laid a trap for him. Simon insulted him and thought God would be pleased with the way he treated Jesus. They thought they knew the woman. They thought they knew how she should behave. They thought they knew misbehavior when they saw it, and they thought they knew that Jesus could never forgive anyone's sins. But every step of the way, they thought wrong!

It is so hard to admit one's errors when one is proud. Even when Jesus told Simon the simple parable he had a hard time telling Jesus the correct answer because to give him the correct answer meant that Jesus was right and he was wrong.

Are you like this man? I pray not. When we walk deeply into pride, it becomes hard to humble oneself before God and to admit that God is right and we are wrong. But humble ourselves we must.

Second, the servants and the bystanders play an important role. The servants have their hands tied. They can do nothing. They have received orders to do nothing for Jesus from their master, Simon. One wonders if a servant had stepped forward how the story might have changed. He surely would have received the wrath of Simon the Pharisee, but he would have received the praise of God.

The same is true of the bystanders. They came into the luncheon area to watch the men eat and to hear their conversation. Perhaps they were curious. Perhaps they were hoping to watch Jesus do another miracle. Perhaps they wanted to hear an argument because they liked a good fight. Are you like the servants and the bystanders? Curious, wanting to see something exciting? Afraid to act when an injustice has been done! Step out in faith! Be courageous. Worship Jesus today.

Then, there was the woman. Perhaps you identify most with her. The woman was the only one who acted. She had courage to step forward when others would not. The woman was willing to shame herself by letting down her hair while others would not even give a towel. But the woman was there as one who had been forgiven much and who deeply loved Jesus. Everyone heard the same message that Jesus gave. But the woman mixed the word of Jesus with faith in her heart. Her life was transformed and heart awakened to the love for which it was created.

Perhaps you have sinned greatly. If you will let the words of Jesus penetrate your heart, you will find your crusty, old heart strangely warmed and renewed by the power of God. You will find yourself coming alive again. You will find your heart filling with love for God. You will have courage. You will not be afraid of what others may say or think about you, so great will be your gratitude for the mercy of Jesus in your life.

The woman who wept at Jesus' feet – it is a story of a woman's deepest desires fulfilled beyond her wildest imaginations. When she had heard Jesus teach earlier in the day her heart had been touched by the love of God and she felt her soul coming alive again as the forgiveness and mercy of God spread through her. She had longed to be close to Jesus and to thank him but she had no idea how she could get close to him.

But at the home of Simon the Pharisee, God opened a door for her to worship Jesus and her honoring him has been told countless times through the ages, and now it has been told to you.

How much Jesus enjoyed what this woman was doing! While the religious people recoiled in revulsion, Jesus received her worship with joy for this sinner had repented and found God. Such will be his response to you, if you will come to him in humility, in gratitude, and in worship. He loves you. He has died for you, and he has risen to be your Lord. He awaits your arrival at his feet to worship.

The Story as Originally Told in Luke 7:36-50

36 Now one of the Pharisees was requesting Him to dine with him, and He entered the Pharisee's house and reclined at the table. 37 And there was a woman in the city who was a sinner; and when she learned that He was reclining at the table in the Pharisee's house, she brought an alabaster vial of perfume, 38 and standing behind Him at His feet, weeping, she began to wet His feet with her tears, and kept wiping them with the hair of her head, and kissing His feet and anointing them with the perfume. 39 Now when the Pharisee who had invited Him saw this, he said to himself, "If this man were a prophet He would know who and what sort of person this woman is who is touching Him, that she is a sinner."

 ^{40} *And Jesus answered him, "Simon, I have something to say to you." And he replied, "Say it, Teacher." ^{41} "A moneylender had two debtors: one owed five hundred denarii, and the other fifty. ^{42} When they were unable to repay, he graciously forgave them both. So which of them will love him more?" ^{43} Simon answered and said, "I suppose the one whom he forgave more." And He said to him, "You have judged correctly." ^{44} Turning toward the woman, He said to Simon, "Do you see this woman? I entered your house; you gave Me no water for My feet, but she has wet My feet with her tears and wiped them with her hair. ^{45} You gave Me no kiss; but she, since the time I came in, has not ceased to kiss My feet. ^{46} You did not anoint My head with oil, but she anointed My feet with perfume. ^{47} For this reason I say to you, her sins, which are many, have been forgiven, for she loved much; but he who is forgiven little, loves little." ^{48} Then He said to her, " Your sins have been forgiven." ^{49} Those who were reclining at the table with Him began to say to themselves, " Who is this man who even forgives sins?" ^{50} And He said to the woman, "Your faith has saved you; go in peace."*

Cultural and Historical Insights

➢ It was common for groups to gather for meals to discuss religious subjects, sometimes late into the night. These groups were called *Haberim*. Sometimes a teacher would attend to present his message for discussion.

➢ People from the village were allowed entrance to observe the meal and listen to the discussion.

➢ If everyone reclined at meal it was a banquet and a special occasion. People were seated by rank and their feet washed and a kiss given. Noblemen were anointed with olive oil which was plentiful and cheap.

➤ If a person did not have his feet washed and was not given a kiss, the audience would immediately pick up on this oversight and would know something was wrong.

➤ If someone were insulted in such a way, it would be customary for that person to reply to the insult with an insult of their own and withdraw from the occasion.

➤ Simon attempted to show Jesus to be of inferior rank by not offering him water, a kiss, or oil.

➤ In the Middle East, a guest would never say anything bad about the hospitality or lack of it offered to him, yet Jesus did this, showing himself to be of superior rank.

➤ Jesus said, "I came under your roof," in other words, "I came under your hospitality but you gave me no water." Jesus did not say, "You failed to wash my feet" because that would have implied that Simon would have had to take the role of a servant. He said instead, "you didn't give me water so that I could wash my own feet."

➤ Jesus said, "You gave me no kiss." Because Simon called him "Teacher" he should have kissed his hand. Students, children, and servants kiss the hand of teachers, parents, masters. Equals kiss on the cheek. But Jesus did not say "you did not kiss me on the hand," only that a kiss was not offered. Again, we see his gentleness toward Simon.

➤ For a woman to let down her hair was to be done only in the presence of a husband at home. It was a public shame and was equal to exposing one's breasts.

➤ Although oil was not provided for Jesus, the woman provided perfume for his feet. She would not presume to carry out these actions on his hands or face but only on his feet. She is humble before him.

> ➤ Simon's revulsion toward the woman shows he has not yet accepted her into the community. Jesus' response frees her from personal sin and brings her back into the community.

These insights gleaned from *Through Peasants' Eyes* by Dr. Kenneth Bailey, 1-21, Eerdmans, 1983.

Reflection

What message do you think the woman heard that prompted her to seek out Jesus? What message from Jesus do you think women need to hear today?

_____

_____

_____

Why do you think Simon the Pharisee insulted Jesus when he entered the banquet hall? Do you believe it was on purpose?

_____

_____

_____

The woman's weeping was so intense that she had enough tears to wash the feet of Jesus. What do you think were all the reasons for her crying?

_____

_____

_____

It was obvious the woman had been deeply touched by Jesus and was truly repentant, yet the Pharisees did not grasp that. What causes people to have such hard hearts that they miss the work of God?

_____

_____

_____

Have you ever wept in the presence of God? If so, what has caused you to weep? Have you ever wept over your sins and failures and over the joy of his forgiveness in your life?

_____

_____

_____

If you could offer something to Jesus, what would it be?

_____

_____

_____

Listen to this story online at http://wgsministries.org/stories/ministry/.
Click on **Follow Me** *(SM011-020)*, scroll down to **The Woman Who
Wept at Jesus Feet – SM020**, and play.

Jonathan Williams

The Bleeding Woman & the Dying Daughter

For twelve years she had suffered. She had consulted with doctors and spent her entire fortune on their remedies – with no help to show. Now she was reduced to poverty and cut off from friends and family. Then she heard the wonderful news, Jesus had come to her town!

Jonathan Williams

2 THE BLEEDING WOMAN & THE DYING DAUGHTER

Jairus was alone in the synagogue, this synagogue where he had led his people in worship of the one true God all of his adult life. He had enjoyed his work and counted it a privilege to have such an esteemed position in his community and to help his people learn the truth about the God of creation who also had entered into a covenant of love with them.

But this time Jairus was not working. He was not preparing for services on the Sabbath or studying what Moses and the Prophets had written. Jairus was praying. All night long Jairus had been in prayer. He was pleading with God for the life of his daughter. She was sick, not getting better, and only God could restore her now.

Hour after hour Jairus prayed, pleaded, begged and asked God to have mercy upon the life of his little girl. She was 12 years old and just getting ready to bloom into the fullness of life. Marriage was only a few years away. She had so much possibility. But the sickness came upon her, and he watched her weaken day after day, life slowing seeping out of her now frail body.

Life was precarious in this part of the world at this time in history. 60% of those born alive were dead by the time they were teens. This 12 year old girl, the daughter who was so loved by her father, would be another who would face the harsh reality of life in a difficult place in the world.

Jairus prayed on and night gave way to day. He could hear people outside the synagogue who had awakened and were now going about their daily tasks. Then he heard footsteps and voices. Two men entered the synagogue. Jairus' heart was filled with dread as he looked at the serious faces of his household servants.

The first servant said, "Jairus, Master, your daughter is not better. We fear for her. You had better come quickly. These may be her last moments."

But the second servant said, "Jairus, Master, some of my fellow servants were out by the lake this morning and they spotted some boats headed this way. When the boats came ashore, inside one of them was Jesus – the healer. He is staying by the seashore teaching but he may come this way, today, to our village. He has healed many people and perhaps he will come and lay his hands upon your daughter."

Jairus was torn. If these were his daughter's last moments he should be by her side. He wanted to be with her. But if this man Jesus could heal her …

Jairus turned to the first man, "Tell my wife I will be there as quickly as I can. I will go to Jesus and ask him to come." Then he turned to the second man, "We have no time to waste. We must go quickly," and away they hurried to find Jesus.

Jesus stayed out by the lake. He was now a famous and

celebrated person. Because not much happened in small villages, whenever anyone of his stature visited, it was a public event. In only a few moments he was recognized and people began to gather around him. Then they heard shouting in the distance.

"Make way! Make way! Jairus, the ruler of our synagogue is coming to see Jesus." The crowd parted to let Jairus through and as he approached many wondered how he would greet Jesus. If two men kissed on the cheek it was a sign they were roughly equal to each other. But if one man bowed on the ground it was a sign of humility before the one who stood.

As Jairus came close he fell to his knees before Jesus and with great earnestness in his voice said, "Jesus, my daughter is dying. She is at the point of death. She is only 12 years old. Oh Jesus, please come and lay your hands upon her that she may live."

Jesus said, "I will come," and the men walked back toward the village. The crowd grew, ten men, twenty men, fifty men, a hundred men. Jesus was surrounded by the men of the village as they entered through its gates and headed in the direction of Jairus' home.

The crowd was excited. They were all headed to see a miracle but many wanted a miracle of their own. Men fought through the crowd to get as close as they could to Jesus. They reached out their hands to grab him, to touch him, anything to receive a blessing from Jesus. The disciples were having trouble controlling the crowd and the road to Jairus' house was clogged with people trying to see Jesus or be near him. Jairus began to be desperate. He knew he had only moments and that his daughter could even be breathing her last as they slowly made their way through the village.

"Didn't these people understand? Didn't these people care?" he thought. But the village men were thinking only of themselves and their needs. They wanted Jesus to come to their homes and help them.

Unknown to all of these men, a shadowy figure lurked in the back of the crowd slowly making progress, step by step getting closer to Jesus. This person had also heard that Jesus was in the village and this person was a woman. Her name is unknown to us. At one point in her life she may have been wealthy, for unlike others she had money to spend on doctors. This woman had a problem. She continuously bled. Her monthly period was not normal and would continue long after it was supposed to stop.

For twelve long years this woman endured this condition. She consulted with one doctor after another – but her condition only worsened. Now she was out of money, living in poverty with no one to care for her.

She had probably never married – for no man in that culture would touch a woman in such a condition. Or, if she had married, undoubtedly her husband had left her. With her condition, a husband would never be able to have sexual relations with her and remain ceremonially clean. He would divorce her for another woman.

But it was not just that she was penniless and unmarried in a place that valued wealth, marriage and children, she was also considered unclean before God and people. She could never visit the Temple in Jerusalem. She could never attend services at the synagogue. She was not allowed to touch others. She was not allowed to sit on furniture others used. If someone accidently brushed up against her or just touched her clothing, they would be considered unclean. She could not share food with others and water in her presence had to be covered up so that it would not become unclean. She was a social outcaste. She was cut off from her people.

But Jesus was coming to her village that day and when she heard it, she made a decision. She would try to find him and be healed.

This was an impossible challenge – not for Jesus – but for her. She was unclean. No one would let her near him. How could she get close to Jesus? And, she was a woman. It was not proper for a woman to speak to a man in public. It was not proper for a woman to touch a man. But the woman was desperate and Jesus was her only hope. If only she could get close to him. If only she could touch him, she believed she would be healed.

She covered herself with a robe and slipped out of her house. One had to look hard to realize she was a woman. That worked to her advantage. Perhaps others would think, if she drew her robe close around her face, that she was a man and in that way she could get in close to Jesus, touch him, be healed, and then make her escape. No one would know that she, an unclean woman, had been around any of them.

It was easy to find Jesus. One just had to listen for the noise of the crowd. But when the woman saw the crowd she was dismayed. She quickly spotted Jesus but how could she get to him? There were a hundred men around him and they were all trying to get to him.

She lowered her voice to mask her identity and asked someone near, "What is happening? Where are they going?" And the person said, "Jairus' daughter is dying. They are going to his house and Jesus said he would heal her but I don't know if they are going to make it in time – that crowd won't let them through."

The woman continued to study the situation. Then she saw it. Toward the rear of the crowd was an opening. Most people were standing to the front of Jesus trying to get Jesus to look at them, trying to get his attention. If she could just slip through the few people that were in back of him, she might be able to get to him and touch his garment. She could pretend to fall and reach down toward his feet and touch the edge of his garment, be healed, then get back up and slip away unnoticed. She knew Jesus could heal her.

As the crowd slowly made its way to the home of Jairus, the woman quietly slipped to the back of the crowd and pulled her robe close around her face. No one noticed her. Good, her plan was working. Step by step, she made her way closer to Jesus. She was bumping against men, each one becoming unclean with her touch, but they didn't know and she didn't care. She had to get to Jesus.

The crowd grew more tense. Loud shouting for people to get out of the way, people crying and screaming, "Jesus come to my house. Jesus help me. Jesus heal me." Hands were clawing to reach him. The disciples were looking concerned, and then, as if something or someone pushed the woman from behind, she stumbled forward through the small group of men at the back of Jesus. She fell to the ground at the feet of Jesus and as he was stepping away she reached out and grabbed the fringe of his robe.

In the next instant she felt it – like lightning coursing through her body – she felt the power of God and she gasped and screamed with fear and then with joy as his power surged through her, and she knew was healed.

In the next moment she heard the voice of Jesus above the crowd.

"Everyone stop! Someone touched me!"

The woman had been discovered. She had been healed as she hoped but her plan to get away and not be recognized had not succeeded. She, an unclean woman, had touched a man and in public!

The crowd stopped and everyone became silent. The disciples said, "Jesus, Master, everyone is touching you. Everyone is grabbing for you. Why do you say that someone has touched you!"

And Jesus replied, "I felt healing power leave my body. Someone touched the edge of my garment and power flowed from me to someone in this crowd. Who touched my garments?"

The woman fell at the feet of Jesus with fear and trembling. She had succeeded in touching him but had not succeeded in getting away. She had been discovered and when Jesus demanded that the one who was healed come forward she had no choice.

"I am the one who touched your garment." Then she pulled back her robe and revealed her long hair and beautiful face and said, "I am a woman." The crowd was shocked. She had done something improper. She, a woman had touched a man in public.

The woman continued. "I know I am not supposed to be in this crowd. I know what others say about my place and where I am supposed to be. But Jesus, I was desperate. For twelve years I have been bleeding. For twelve years I have been unclean. I have consulted with physician after physician and no one has helped. I have only grown worse. I have lost all my money and am down to nothing. I have not been able to be with my family. I have not been able to touch another. I have not felt the hug of a friend or the kiss of a loved one and I thought if I could only just touch the edge of your robe I would be healed. I am the one who touched you."

The village men wondered what Jesus would do. She had interrupted a gathering led by the synagogue leader. She, an unclean woman has touched a religious teacher. Jesus was famous. She was a nobody, poor and destitute. Jesus was a righteous man. She was a religiously unclean woman. And she had slowed down the procession to heal the daughter of the synagogue leader. She had broken all the rules of decency, purity, and honor in her village.

The men wondered, "What will Jesus do? What will he say to her? Will he condemn her for breaking the social barriers? Will he condemn her for touching him?" But they were not prepared for the scene that would unfold before them and the words he would say to the woman who was weeping and trembling with fear over what she had done.

Jesus knelt beside the woman who was on her face and he said, "Daughter, take courage! Your faith has made you well. Go in peace, and be healed of your affliction."

The men could not believe their ears. The woman could not believe her ears. Jesus was not condemning her. Jesus was blessing her. He had healed her body and now he pronounced a blessing of peace upon her spirit. And what did he called her? "Daughter?" She belonged again! She belonged to Jesus! She belonged to God and now she could belong to her family again and to her village!

Jesus helped the woman to her feet and motioned for the crowd to part and let her pass. This time, as she walked she did not have to lurk in the shadows. This time, as she walked she did not have to gather her robe around her face and hide her identity. This time she could walk freely and openly. She took one more look at Jesus whose reassuring smile filled her with joy and went home.

The crowd stood still and in silence. Many wondered why they had not been healed. They had touched Jesus' body and nothing happened. She had touched the fringe of his garment and was healed. What had Jesus said about faith?

Just then a man came running up to the crowd and with sorrow in voice said, "Where is Jairus? I must see Jairus. I have a message for him." They took the man to Jairus who was standing with Jesus' disciples as Jesus sent the woman away and the man said, "Jairus, I am so sorry. But your daughter is gone. She is dead. Jesus is too late. Do not trouble him anymore."

Grief and anguish filled Jairus' heart. If only the crowd had been more cooperative they might have made it in time. If only the woman had not interrupted they might have been at his home before his daughter breathed her last.

But Jesus heard what the man had said to Jairus and he turned to him and said, "Jairus, do not be afraid! Only believe and she will

This time, as she walked she did not have to lurk in the shadows. This time, as she walked she did not have to gather her robe around her face and hide her identity. This time she could walk freely and openly. She took one more look at Jesus whose reassuring smile filled her with joy and went home.

be made well."

Jesus turned to the crowd and said, "All of you – go home! Peter, James, John – come with me." And this time Jairus and Jesus and three of Jesus' disciples made their way through the crowd without any delay.

When they came to the house, it was already filling with people. Flute players were playing their sad melodies. Tambourine players were beating their somber beat of sorrow. Professional mourners were loudly wailing and crying. The house was filled with noise and disorder and commotion, just like the crowd a few moments earlier in the village and Jesus in a loud voice said:

"Why are you making all of this noise and commotion. The girl has not died. She only sleeps. Please, all of you leave. Go home."

The crowd was stunned. They grew quiet, and then they burst into laughter. Whereas only a moment before they were weeping, now they were laughing with scorn at this man who had the audacity to come into the home of the synagogue leader whose daughter had just died and say that she was not dead. Who did he think he was? Didn't he know what was proper? Didn't he know their place as official mourners? How could he be so cruel to say that Jairus' daughter was only asleep?

But as they laughed with scorn Jairus said, "Do as he says," and he, Jesus, and Jesus' disciples put all the people out of the house.

Then Jesus said, "Take me to her," and Jairus and his wife took Jesus to their daughter. She looked so peaceful. She did look like she was asleep. But her face was pale and the color continued to drain from her sweet face.

Jesus walked to the girl. He knelt beside her bed. He looked upon her features and thought how his Father had made her for his glory. He thought upon the father and mother who had brought her into the world and raised her with joy and hope. Then, he took her by the hand and gently said, "Little girl, I say to you, rise up!" and immediately the girl's spirit returned to her body. She took a deep breath which startled her father and mother, opened her eyes, and looked upon Jesus. Then she sat up and taking Jesus by the hand began to walk about the room.

Jesus said, "Give her something to eat. She will be weak and needs nourishment."

The parents were astounded. They could not believe their eyes. Their beloved daughter was alive and well. God had heard Jairus' prayers and had mercy upon his daughter!

As Jairus and his wife embraced their little girl with joy, they thanked Jesus, and as she ate and walked about the room exercising her weak legs Jesus turned to Jairus and said, "Don't tell anyone what I have done." Then Jesus and Peter, James, and John left the house while eyes from the village people looked upon them with scorn and suspicion.

It was impossible to keep the secret. In the days to come, as the girl began to grow stronger, she was soon about the house and around the village with her parents and people knew what had happened. The girl who had died had come back to life, and the news went out into all the land.

~~~

The stories of the dying daughter who was resurrected and the bleeding woman who was healed have now gone out into all the world for the Jesus who raised the girl and the Jesus who healed the woman is Lord of all. Jesus is the Savior of the world and he has come to bring the power, mercy, and love of the reign of God from heaven to earth. Now that he has died for our sins and been raised he has sent his followers into all the world to tell these stories and to tell the great story of his love for you.

I must ask you this question. As you think on these stories, who are you most like? Are you like the crowd around Jesus that pushed and shoved and tried to get close? Are you like the ones who did touch him but had nothing happen for them, or, are you like the woman who had faith and who said, "If I only touch the edge of his robe I will be healed"?

Are you like the crowd that was making loud noise with crying and mournful music when the little girl died, or are you like Jairus who believed Jesus' word when he said, "Do not be afraid. Only believe"?

Jesus has come into the world to bring the reign of God, the kingdom of God to mankind. He wishes to reign as your Lord and Savior, but he will only reign where he finds faith. And so I ask you today, are you full of noise, full of busyness, full of pushing and shoving in life, full of grief and mourning and fear, or, are you full of faith and reaching out to touch the edge of his robes?

Read the Story as Originally Told in Mark 5:21-43

[21]When Jesus had crossed over again in the boat to the other side, a large crowd gathered around Him; and so He stayed by the seashore. [22] One of the synagogue officials named Jairus came up,

and on seeing Him, fell at His feet ^{23} and implored Him earnestly, saying, "My little daughter is at the point of death; please come and lay Your hands on her, so that she will get well and live." ^{24} And He went off with him; and a large crowd was following Him and pressing in on Him.

^{25} A woman who had had a hemorrhage for twelve years, ^{26} and had endured much at the hands of many physicians, and had spent all that she had and was not helped at all, but rather had grown worse— ^{27} after hearing about Jesus, she came up in the crowd behind Him and touched His cloak. ^{28} For she thought, "If I just touch His garments, I will get well." ^{29} Immediately the flow of her blood was dried up; and she felt in her body that she was healed of her affliction. ^{30} Immediately Jesus, perceiving in Himself that the power proceeding from Him had gone forth, turned around in the crowd and said, "Who touched My garments?" ^{31} And His disciples said to Him, "You see the crowd pressing in on You, and You say, 'Who touched Me?'" ^{32} And He looked around to see the woman who had done this. ^{33} But the woman fearing and trembling, aware of what had happened to her, came and fell down before Him and told Him the whole truth. ^{34} And He said to her, "Daughter, your faith has made you well; go in peace and be healed of your affliction."

^{35} While He was still speaking, they came from the house of the synagogue official, saying, "Your daughter has died; why trouble the Teacher anymore?" ^{36} But Jesus, overhearing what was being spoken, said to the synagogue official, " Do not be afraid any longer, only believe." ^{37} And He allowed no one to accompany Him, except Peter and James and John the brother of James. ^{38} They came to the house of the synagogue official; and He saw a commotion, and people loudly weeping and wailing. ^{39} And *entering in, He said to them, "Why make a commotion and weep? The child has not died, but is asleep."* [40] *They began laughing at Him. But putting them all out, He took along the child's father and mother and His own companions, and entered the room where the child was.* [41] *Taking the child by the hand, He said to her, "Talitha kum!" (which translated means, "Little girl, I say to you, get up!").* [42] *Immediately the girl got up and began to walk, for she was twelve years old. And immediately they were completely astounded.* [43] *And He gave them strict orders that no one should know about this, and He said that something should be given her to eat.*

Cultural and Historical Insights

➤ In Western culture, people are public about sex and private about a woman's menstruation. In the Middle East they are private about sex and public about menstruation.

➤ Normally, upon entering a village, the elders would welcome a person such as Jesus and offer hospitality because he would be a celebrity. The elders would meet him, invite him to a meal to show respect, and he would accept the invitation to show respect to them.

➤ In this story, Jesus is greeted by a synagogue leader whose daughter is at the point of death. Medicine was primitive and divine healing hoped for. Jesus' healing was extraordinary because he did not use magic formulas or incantations.

➤ Jesus was surrounded by crowds. Little that was new happened in these villages. When an outsider, especially a celebrity like Jesus entered, the entire village would know. In such a situation, events would become public.

- The crowd would be composed mostly of men and strict boundaries between men and women existed. For a woman to touch a man was highly irregular. Such a woman would barely look at a man and would not speak to one who was not part of her family.
- The woman had uterine or menstrual bleeding. This made her religiously impure. A woman who was having her period was considered impure. See Leviticus 15:20-23 for the regulations.
- What Romans believed (from Pliny) – "Contact with the monthly flow of a woman would turn new wine sour, make crops wither, kill skin grafts, dry seeds in gardens, cause fruit to fall from trees, dim the surface of mirrors, dull the edge of the sword and the gleam of ivory, kill bees, and rust iron and bronze. Dogs that came near went insane and their bite became poisonous. One thread from one garment worn by such a woman would do this. She could turn linen black by touching it, but she could drive away hailstorms and whirlwinds if she showed herself unclothed when lightning flashed. If she walked through a field with her robe above her belt, bugs would fall off the ears of corn, but she must not do this at sunrise or the crops would die." This is how people thought! Thus, a woman such as she was would cause anxiety in a crowd, and it would reinforce her isolation.
- Only the elite had money to spend on physicians. The woman in the story may have been an elite woman who was reduced to poverty for she spent all she had.
- In Israel, men wore ankle length robes or tunics. Religious men were distinguished by the bottom fringe of their tunic which would have tassels as a reminder to keep the Law of God. These were strings that hung from the four corners of the garment and they would have one blue thread as a reminder to obey the Law. Jesus wore such a garment.

> Reaching for the fringe of the garment is to reach for a part of the garment that symbolizes authority as a religious man with spiritual authority.

> When Jesus arrived at Jairus' home, the mourners were there. Culture required at least two flute players and one professional mourner. But Jairus was a respected and well known man and many others would be there to cry and to perform dances of mourning.

> A 12-year old dying would be common. In the first century 60% of those born alive had died by their mid teens.

Cultural and historical insights taken from *Social-Science Commentary on the Synoptic Gospels*, Bruce J. Malina, Fortress Press, 61-62, 395-397 and *Encounters with Jesus* by Gary M. Burge, Zondervan, 39-53.

Reflection

The bleeding woman had to be desperate and courageous to approach Jesus and touch him. Have you known anyone this desperate and/or courageous in following Jesus?

_____

_____

_____

Jesus had just returned from an unclean place inhabited by gentiles. We read about this in Mark 5:1-20. It was a place of death (the tombs), he met a demonized man, and there were pigs in the area. When he returned to the western side of the Sea of Galilee he is touched by an unclean woman and then touches a dead girl. What message do you think the Gospel writers are conveying by Jesus' frequent interaction with "unclean" people and things?

_____

_____

_____

Jesus told the woman that her faith had made her well. In how many different ways did she show faith in this story?

_____

_____

_____

_____

Jesus told Jairus not to fear but only to believe. In what ways did Jairus show faith after he was told that his daughter was dead?

_____

_____

_____

Why do you think Jesus told Jairus and his family to tell no one about the resurrection of the daughter? How could they have kept it a secret?

_____

_____

_____

In what ways can you show faith in Jesus in your life?

_____

_____

_____

Listen to this story online at http://wgsministries.org/stories/ministry/. Click on **Who Do Men Say That I Am?** *(SM021-030)*, scroll down to **The Bleeding Woman and the Dying Daughter – SM024**, and play.

Crumbs from the Master's Table

A little girl was possessed by an evil spirit who brought untold suffering to her and her family. When her mother heard Jesus was nearby, she sought him out for help only to discover he was not there to heal. Then, she said something that moved Jesus' heart to fulfill her bold request.

Jonathan Williams

3 CRUMBS FROM THE MASTER'S TABLE

Pressure was coming from every quarter. The political leaders of the land had heard of Jesus and his mighty works of power and were concerned about insurrection in the land. The religious leaders had sent delegations to question him and found his activities scandalous and dangerous. They believed he was leading the people astray. His family members at times thought he had lost his mind. The crowds wanted to crown him as their king but their kind of kingdom was different from the kind of kingdom God wanted. And often even his own disciples did not fully understand his mission. Yes, pressure was coming from every quarter, and it was time to take a break.

Jesus and his disciples had tried to get away several days previous to this. The disciples had just returned from their own preaching tour and needed a rest. They got into a boat and sailed to a spot on the shore of the Sea of Galilee where they thought no one would be, but word got out about their destination and they were greeted by thousands! Jesus graciously spent time with them, teaching, healing, and feeding the thousands. But it was time to give it another try, and this time Jesus and the disciples did something they rarely did, they left the borders of Israel.

They went northwest from Galilee in Israel into the region of Tyre and Sidon, major cities in the land of the Phoenicians and Syrians. This was a hilly area where few people lived and the prospect for some days of rest and quiet seemed almost certain.

The land of the Phoenicians and Syrians had played a role in the history of God's people. When King David built a palace for himself, he used workers from this area who were experts in construction, and the wood from this area was some of the best in the world for such building projects. Solomon also used their craftsmanship in the building of the great temple. This was a wealthy land and the people of Tyre had been a great sea power for centuries, trading with other nations, and even colonizing distant lands. Now, in the time of Jesus the area was inhabited by many sophisticated Greek people who were aligned with Roman imperial policy. Rome was the new power and Rome afforded protection for their land and wealth.

It was also a land of great spiritual darkness and need. Rome could give military protection. The Greeks could bring their wealth and philosophy, but neither could satisfy the hunger of men's hearts for a relationship with the true God. Neither could provide solutions for the deep spiritual needs of the people. In this land lived a woman and her daughter, and their needs were great.

We are not told if she was married, a single mother, a widow, or divorced. What we know is that she had a child, a daughter, and something was wrong with her little girl. The woman believed she was afflicted with an evil spirit. We are not told what this spirit did to the child, but only that it caused cruel suffering for the child.

That this woman heard about Jesus is not surprising. Even though Jesus confined his work to Israel, news about his healing power spread far beyond the borders of Israel. Matthew tells us the news about Jesus spread throughout all Syria and that people brought to Him all who were ill, those suffering with various diseases and pains, demoniacs, epileptics, paralytics, and he healed them all! As people would return to their homes with great joy they would also return with the news of this great man who had power and compassion for everyone.

For some reason the woman had never been able to travel to see this Jesus. But one day she heard something that brought hope to her troubled heart – Jesus was in the area! Jesus had come to her land! How she discovered this, no one knows, but the woman set off at once to find Jesus.

If, somehow, we could see this scene from above, we would see a woman traveling southeast in the direction of Israel and she is looking for Jesus. We would also see a group of men travelling northwest away from Israel and they are looking for privacy and quiet. A woman is travelling with great need in her heart – she is burdened for her daughter who is afflicted with an evil spirit. Jesus is travelling with great need in his heart – he is burdened for the world but he also needs time to rest and find refreshment for the great work ahead. Their paths would soon meet in one of the greatest stories of faith ever told.

Jesus and his disciples entered a small village. They made some inquiries and found a home they could use for a few days. Jesus entered the home and he told his disciples, "Please, don't let anyone know that I am here."

But the woman was in the same village and she was asking everyone, "Please, I am looking for Jesus. I have heard that he is here. I am speaking of Jesus, from Nazareth in Galilee. He is the one who has healing power. Do you know where he is?" Finally the woman comes across the people who are letting Jesus use their home for a few days and they say, "Yes, he is using our home – look, just down at the end of the road. You can see some of his followers standing outside the home. In fact, I think Jesus has just come outside to speak with them. But I don't think he wants to be disturbed, I think …"

But the woman did not hear the man. She immediately set off as fast as she could and when she saw Jesus she immediately started crying out, "Have mercy on me, Lord, Son of David, my daughter is cruelly afflicted with an evil spirit. Jesus, please, help me. My daughter is so sick."

But Jesus didn't say a word. He just stared at the woman in her pitiful state as she continued crying and asking for mercy with a loud voice. "Have mercy on me, Lord, Son of David, my daughter is cruelly afflicted with an evil spirit. Jesus, please, help me."

The disciples could not believe it! They had been discovered again! Was this going to be like the Sea of Galilee where they tried to get away for a few days of rest only to find thousands of people waiting for them? This was only one person but she was making so much noise, others would hear and a crowd would soon form.

As the woman continued shouting, some of Jesus' disciples said, "Master, send her away. You sent the crowds away in Galilee. This is just one woman. Send her away. Look down the street, people can hear her and soon the whole village will know you are here. Lord, heal her daughter and send her away and then get back in the house. Do something before this time is ruined too!"

But Jesus said to his disciples. "You want me to heal her just to quiet her and then send her away? No, I will not. Besides, in the ministry that my Father has given me for this time, I was sent only to the lost sheep of Israel. This woman is not of Israel. It is not yet time for her."

But the woman had overheard what Jesus said and she came up to him and fell at his feet and said, "Jesus, please, help me. Lord, help me!"

And Jesus said to her, "Woman, when a family prepares a meal, do they take the food and share it with the little puppies that are around the house, or do they feed their children first? It is not good to take away the food that belongs to the children and give it to the dogs."

But the woman said, "Yes, Lord, that is true. But sometimes, the little dogs are under the table, and when crumbs of food fall from the table while everyone is eating, they eat those crumbs and are satisfied."

A huge smile filled the face of Jesus and his heart leaped with joy over her words. This is what he was looking for in the hearts of his people – this kind of humble faith. Jesus closed his eyes. He saw the little girl lying on her bed of sickness. He also saw the spirit that afflicted her and when the spirit saw him terror filled its heart. Then, the spirit heard words of power and authority come to it from the heart of Jesus, "Be gone." And immediately the evil spirit obeyed and left her.

Jesus said to the woman, "O woman, because of your answer, because of your words of faith, the demon has gone out of your daughter." And the woman stood up, wiped the tears from her face and walked away. When she returned home, she found her child resting upon her bed with a look of peace upon her sweet face, for the demon had gone, never to return.

~~~

There is so much to learn from this story. Why did Jesus say he was sent only to Israel? Was he not sent for the whole world? Why did Jesus say that he did not want to give food to the dogs? Was he calling the woman, or the woman's child, a dog? And then, why did he heal the woman's daughter? What was it in her words that moved Jesus to perform his work of power for her, especially at this time when he was seeking to avoid people?

There were so many obstacles the woman had to overcome.

First, Jesus was in her village, but he did not come to teach, to feed people, or to heal. He came for some much needed rest. She wanted help. He was there for quiet and rest.

Second, when the woman first started crying out, Jesus did not say a word. He did not immediately heal the girl but kept quiet, reminding us that sometimes God is silent to us. But his silence is never a sign that he does not love us. To this woman it must have been a concern that Jesus seemed unmoved, at first, by her pleas. In the same way, we can grow concerned when it seems he is unmoved by our plight and by our cries for help.

Third, Jesus' disciples wanted to send her away. There wasn't much love coming from these men. They had learned many lessons but they still had much to learn about ministry to people. They said, "Lord, send her away! Just, show your power and have her leave so we can have this time to ourselves." How did that make her feel? How does that make you feel when people just want to get rid of you because you are an inconvenience or interrupting them?

But the attitude of the disciples, Jesus' silence, and the fact that

Jesus had not come to heal did not stop the woman. She persevered, stayed right in front of Jesus and found the miracle for which she had come.

Fourth, Jesus said, "I was sent only to the lost sheep of the house of Israel." What did Jesus mean? Did he not care for the gentiles as well as the Jews? Had he not come for the whole world? He had indeed come for the whole world, but first, he had to come for Israel because the prophecies said that first Israel must be saved, then the message of salvation would go to the world through the restored nation. When the woman heard Jesus' words, she knew she was not of Israel and that it was not her time. Yet, she did not leave. She stayed and continued pleading with Jesus. She had to have the blessing of God in her life.

When the woman came and knelt before Jesus, like a little lost puppy, whimpering for her sad state and that of her daughter, Jesus said it was not good to take the children's bread and give it to the dogs. Some have thought Jesus was insulting her. In that part of the world, at that time in history, dogs were mean scavengers and were not usually household pets. They roamed in packs and were considered unclean and dangerous. If a household did have a dog as a pet, the dog would only receive the scraps from the dinner table after everyone had eaten.

Food was hard to come by for many. There were not modern stores with brightly colored packages of dog food as we have today in some parts of the world. The dogs ate the leftovers after everyone in the family had eaten. Sometimes, the dogs would sit under the table. On lucky days food would fall from the table and they were there to gobble it up.

As the woman thought on how children ate first, even in her own family, and then the dogs, she thought on the many times that dogs would sit under the table and on some lucky days some food would fall from the table and they would hungrily eat.

The woman thought on something else. She thought on Jesus and his greatness. Yes, it is true that it was not time for the gentiles, but was not Jesus greater? She thought on how it was not yet time to feed the rest of the world and that first he must feed his own people. But was not Jesus' power great enough to provide for others even at this time? If she could have just a crumb, just a small portion, that would be enough for her. She did not need a full meal, just a crumb would be enough, and when the woman spoke her words, Jesus marveled at her great faith.

How many times had Jesus given a full meal to his own people yet they would not believe? How many times had Jesus shown great power to heal but Israel still would not believe? Here was a gentile woman and all she needed was a crumb from the table, not even a full loaf of bread, just a crumb, and she said that would be enough.

When this gentile woman spoke these words she showed great faith, and Jesus leaped over all the obstacles that had been set between him and the woman and healed her daughter. Yes, it was true that he was not there to heal. Yes, it was true that she was a gentile and his focus was still on Israel, but Jesus gladly set that aside because there was a greater lesson for everyone to hear – the lesson of having faith in him.

This was a hard lesson for his people to learn. Strangely, gentiles, women, the blind – those in greatest need – often showed the greatest faith. Once, a Roman soldier wanted Jesus to heal his servant and he showed great faith by his attitude and his words.

Jesus marveled and said, "I have not found such faith in all Israel!" Here was a Roman, a centurion – a leader of a hundred soldiers who were the oppressors of God's people, yet in this Roman, Jesus found faith.

Remember the unclean woman who had the bleeding problem? She was desperate for healing and while everyone else was touching Jesus, grabbing him, wanting healing and receiving nothing, she touched the edge of his robes and immediately was healed. When Jesus had the woman come forward to tell everyone what she had done, he said to her, "Woman, your faith has healed you."

The edge of his robe, a crumb from his table. Healing is no problem for Jesus. It takes very little effort for him, but Jesus came for more than healing. Jesus came to create faith in the hearts of people, and when anyone showed great faith, Jesus was ready to show his power on their behalf to reinforce this vital lesson. Jesus often healed without people showing faith because he was merciful, but what he was looking for among his people was faith. And when anyone showed faith, Jesus was ready to act. When this woman showed her faith in Jesus, her daughter was immediately released from the evil spirit.

Why is faith so important to Jesus? Faith is a demonstration of a good relationship, and faith shows the trustworthiness of the one in whom the faith is placed.

Think of your relationships. Think of the people you trust and those you do not. The ones that you trust – why do you trust them? The ones that you do not – why do you not trust them? With whom do you have the best relationships? Who are the ones you keep at arms length, the ones you don't care for? These questions are easily answered. Trust-filled relationships are the ones we hold close to us. They are the kind of relationships we all want.

God wants to have a trust filled relationship with us. He wants us to realize that we can trust him. He does love us. He does have our best in mind. He will work out all things for good for those who love him. God does not want to be some religious figurehead in our minds. God does not want to be just a concept and someone we refer to once a week when we attend religious services. He wants us to trust him, and he wants us to be trustworthy and open with him and to do what he wants us to do.

Second, faith shows the trustworthiness of the person in whom you are placing faith. When you place faith in someone, you are declaring to the world that this person is trust-worthy. They are worthy of you placing your complete faith in them. God wants us to have faith in him and show the world his complete trust-worthiness.

There are other reasons why God wants faith from us. Only by faith can we see what God wants to make of us, and only by faith can we move the mountains that stand in the path to doing God's will. Do you have mountains in your life? Do you have obstacles you cannot seem to get over? Think of this woman from the region of Syria and Phoenicia. Think of her troubles. Think of the obstacles she had to overcome and think of the persevering faith she had in Jesus, so strong, so steadfast, that Jesus met her great faith with a great work of power for her daughter.

Throughout his ministry, Jesus was seeking for trust-filled relationships and Jesus was seeking to build faith in his disciples. These men would need great faith to carry out the mission that he would send them on after he died and rose from the dead. Even though, during their years together in Israel, it was not time for the mission to the gentiles, that time would come when he would send them out to all the nations of the world and they would need great faith for their journeys. And so, during their time of ministry together, Jesus would point out to them the faith of others – like this woman, "O woman, your faith is great." He would reprove them for their unbelief. When Peter started walking on water, then took his eyes off Jesus and started to sink, Jesus said, "O you of little faith!" At other times he would place them into situations that required faith. When Jesus stilled the storm on the Sea of Galilee he said to them all, "where is your faith!"

What about you? What kind of faith do you have? Do you have a trust-filled relationship with Jesus? Jesus came to this earth, died on the cross, rose from the dead, and sent those same disciples – who wanted to send the woman away – out into the world to people just like the woman that they might share the good news that God was searching for people with whom he could have a trust-filled relationship.

~~~

After Jesus healed the woman's daughter he and his followers left the area. They travelled along the northern part of the Sea of Galilee and into the region to the east which was another gentile area. Jesus healed a deaf man and word spread of his presence.

Thousands came to him again, and again they had no food except seven loaves of bread and a few small fish. What was this among four thousand men? But this time the disciples were ready! At Jesus' command, the disciples had everyone recline and Jesus broke the bread and the fish and the disciples served all the people in this region of the gentiles on the eastern side of the Sea of Galilee.

Jesus watched as his men served the food. A day would come when they would serve the true, spiritual food to the multitudes, not only here, but everywhere in the world. As Jesus watched his men serve the bread, and as he watched 4000 men hungrily partake of it, did he think of the woman who needed only a crumb from his table to find healing for her daughter? Did Jesus think of the trust filled relationship that he had built with her? Did he think of the trust filled relationships he would build with millions of people in the ages to come? Was he thinking of you?

Read the Story as Originally Told in Matthew 15:21-39

21 Jesus went away from there, and withdrew into the district of Tyre and Sidon. 22 And a Canaanite woman from that region came out and began to cry out, saying, "Have mercy on me, Lord, Son of David; my daughter is cruelly demon-possessed." 23 But He did not answer her a word. And His disciples came and implored Him, saying, "Send her away, because she keeps shouting at us." 24 But He answered and said, "I was sent only to the lost sheep of the house of Israel." 25 But she came and began to bow down before Him, saying, "Lord, help me!" 26 And He answered and said, "It is not good to take the children's bread and throw it to the dogs."

²⁷ *But she said, "Yes, Lord; but even the dogs feed on the crumbs which fall from their masters' table." ²⁸ Then Jesus said to her, "O woman, your faith is great; it shall be done for you as you wish." And her daughter was healed at once.*

²⁹ *Departing from there, Jesus went along by the Sea of Galilee, and having gone up on the mountain, He was sitting there. ³⁰ And large crowds came to Him, bringing with them those who were lame, crippled, blind, mute, and many others, and they laid them down at His feet; and He healed them. ³¹ So the crowd marveled as they saw the mute speaking, the crippled restored, and the lame walking, and the blind seeing; and they glorified the God of Israel.*

³² *And Jesus called His disciples to Him, and said, "I feel compassion for the people, because they have remained with Me now three days and have nothing to eat; and I do not want to send them away hungry, for they might faint on the way." ³³ The disciples said to Him, "Where would we get so many loaves in this desolate place to satisfy such a large crowd?" ³⁴ And Jesus said to them, "How many loaves do you have?" And they said, "Seven, and a few small fish." ³⁵ And He directed the people to sit down on the ground; ³⁶ and He took the seven loaves and the fish; and giving thanks, He broke them and started giving them to the disciples, and the disciples gave them to the people ³⁷ And they all ate and were satisfied, and they picked up what was left over of the broken pieces, seven large baskets full. ³⁸ And those who ate were four thousand men, besides women and children. ³⁹ And sending away the crowds, Jesus got into the boat and came to the region of Magadan.*

Cultural and Historical Insights

➤ This story is the only record of Jesus addressing a gentile outside the borders of Israel.

➤ The woman lived in modern day Lebanon. These were wealthy Greek areas, and the people who lived here were devoted to the cause of spreading the Roman Empire in these regions. The people who lived in this area knew of Judea to the south but the Judeans were seen as culturally backwards and provincial.

➤ Tyre was the southernmost coastal city of Syrophoenicia.

➤ The people of this land helped build David's palace (2 Samuel 5:11) and Solomon's temple (1 Kings 5:16-20).

➤ Alexander the Great conquered the mainland city in 332 BC and used the rubble to build a causeway to the island city which he also conquered. Then he made it a new important Greek seaport.

➤ Matthew's story calls her a Canaanite woman which referred to the people who lived along the northern coasts. Mark says she is a Syrophonenican woman, i.e., from that province.

➤ Dogs in first century Judaism were scavengers. They roamed in packs outside villages and would eat garbage, dung, and corpses. They were rarely pets and Jews compared them to pigs and considered them unclean – See Isaiah 66:3 and 2 Peter 2:22 for references. They were looked upon with contempt and became a metaphor for things to be despised (see Matthew 7:6).

➤ By her words she shows three things: Respect – she calls him "Lord," or "Master." Knowledge – she calls him Son of David and shows she knows something of Judaism. Character – she asks for mercy and she knows Jesus is generous.

These insights were taken from *Encounters with Jesus* by Gary Burge, Zondervan, 111-125.

Reflection

In several places, the Gospels mention that Jesus would often get alone to pray or rest. What does this say about Jesus' humanity and the needs in his life as a man?

_____

_____

_____

Why do you think Jesus said nothing to the woman at first?

_____

_____

_____

Jesus said he was sent only to the lost sheep of Israel. How does this compare to John 3:16? Is there a timing factor involved in his ministry to Israel and the nations?

_____

_____

_____

Jesus said the woman showed great faith by what she said. How did her words demonstrate great faith? Do our words show faith in Jesus or unbelief?

_____

_____

_____

Do you have any desperate needs in your life, or do you know someone with a desperate need who needs to take them to Jesus?

_____

_____

_____

Listen to this story online at http://wgsministries.org/stories/ministry/. Click on **Who Do Men Say That I Am?** *(SM021-030)*, scroll down to **Crumbs from the Master's Table – SM028**, and play.

The Thirsty Woman – Part 1

Disappointment, then shame, then numbness. She didn't care anymore what others thought. One day she was startled by a Jewish man who spoke with her, revealed the secrets of her heart, and awakened hope within.

4 THE THIRSTY WOMAN – PART 1

She was thirsty, and taking her large pitcher she headed for the well outside the village. She made sure she would be at the well when the other women were not there. They were not her friends because of the life she had lived ... and still lived.

The village was Sychar in the province of Samaria, and it had a rich tradition in which the people had taken much pride. In this area the great patriarch of Israel, Jacob, gave his son Joseph a piece of land. He also dug a well at that site many centuries before. It was to this well, this ancient well, hallowed by Jacob, that the people of the village of Sychar had gone for their water for generations untold.

As the woman trod the familiar path to the well outside the village, she ignored the stares of others who despised her. She was familiar with it. Life had not turned out the way she had hoped when she was a little girl. The dreams of a happy family life and enjoying the friendship of others was just that – only dreams. Far too much had happened through the years to rescue them. Life had settled into an endurance trial – simply surviving one day after another – with little purpose, little joy, and no peace.

At least there would be some solitude at Sychar's well. Every insult that could be said to her had been said. Now she looked forward to being alone where she could snatch some serenity from the peaceful surroundings.

But as she approached she noticed someone was there, a man, and by his dress, a Jewish man. "I wonder," she thought, "if he is connected with the other Jewish men I just passed in the village buying food? That was strange enough. And now here is another Jewish man." It didn't matter. He was a man and she was a woman – there would be little conversation, if any, and besides, he was a Jew and she was a Samaritan. An upright Jewish man would have no dealings with a Samaritan woman. Did not the Jews believe Samaritan women were unclean from the cradle? She laughed at the thought of such Jewish, male-dominated nonsense.

The woman came to the well and set her pitcher down as if he were not there. She started to draw water from the depths when the Jewish man startled her.

"Give me a drink."

The woman stopped. She stared at the man for a few moments and then went back to her task at the well. With a slight edge to her voice she said,

"You are a Jewish man. I am a woman and a Samaritan. Why are you asking me for a drink?"

And the man said, "If you knew the gift of God and the one who is asking you for a drink, you would ask him and he would give you living water."

"Living water?" the woman thought. "How could he supply that?"

The thirsty woman knew this Jewish man was claiming some kind of special power. Living water was the rainfall of God falling into streams and lakes. It was used in ceremonies to make people clean before God. How could this man supply living water which came directly from God? There were no streams or lakes within miles of the village. The man had no jar. He had no water of any kind she could see. What was he talking about? The woman, well experienced in her dealings with men, decided to play along with this one and said,

"Sir, you have nothing to draw water with, and the well is deep. Where do you get your living water? You are not claiming to be greater than our father Jacob are you? You know that he gave us this well and drank from it himself with his sons and with all their cattle. This is a special place. Where do you get your living water?"

The man peered down into Jacob's well, then looked up at the woman and said, "Everyone who drinks from this well will thirst again. They will come back again and again to get water that can never quench the true thirst of man. Whoever drinks of the water that I give shall never thirst again. The water that I give will become – in the one who drinks – a well of water that springs up to eternal life."

The woman looked at the man and thought about her life. How often had she trudged this path and endured the shame that others threw upon her for her lifestyle. How nice it would be to find another source of water that would forever quench her thirst and those with her. Who knows, it might even make her clean before God, if that were possible, and so she said,

"Sir, give me this water so that I will never thirst again and not have to come all the way here to this village well to get water for my family."

Stop! Stop the story! I want you to imagine something with me for a moment. I have been telling you a famous Bible story usually called *The Woman at the Well.* We find it in John 4. Although we never learn the name of the woman, we know who the man is. The woman is talking with Jesus.

Imagine with me that this story as we know it today does not exist. Imagine that the Gospel of John from which it is taken does not exist. Imagine also that you and I are on an archaeological expedition in the Middle East and we make a stupendous discovery. We discover a manuscript that has this story, but the story ends at this point where the woman asks Jesus for his water.

What would your impression be if you had this fragment of the story and nothing more? I know what I would think. I would think that Jesus was having a positive impact with her. I would think that Jesus has made great progress in helping her understand her deep spiritual need. I would think that she is ready to hear about eternal life.

Look at what Jesus had done so far. He had already overcome a social barrier – a man talking with a woman in public. He had already overcome a cultural barrier – a Jew is having a conversation with a Samaritan. He wisely turned the conversation from physical water to living, spiritual water and when the woman heard what he said, she replied that she wanted this living water of which Jesus spoke.

It all sounds so good. If you and I had an encounter like this with someone we might think, "This person is very interested in the things of God and is very close to finding God." But we would be so wrong! Thankfully, we have the entire story, and in the rest of it we will discover what is really going on in the heart of this woman, and what may be going on in our hearts as well.

The woman said to him, " Sir, give me this water so that I will never thirst again and not have to come all the way here to this village well to get water for my family."

And he told her, "Go, call your husband and come back."

Husband? The statement pierced to the depth of the woman's heart and to all her pain. She did not want to go there in this discussion. She wanted the living water Jesus offered, but why did he have to bring up this subject? He had no idea what she had been through. He had no idea how her feelings had been crushed by man after man who only seemed to want one thing.

She thought quickly. How could she avoid this? She cleverly said, "I have no husband."

The woman looked at Jesus, searching his face to see if her clever response would be enough to divert him from probing further into her private life. But her cleverness was no match for the one to whom she spoke, and Jesus said:

"You are right when you say you have no husband. You are quite right! The fact is, you have had five husbands, and the man you are living with now is not your husband. What you have just said is quite true."

Oh ... things are a little more complicated than we first thought. Now we see she doesn't really want all that he offers. She just wants a convenience to make her difficult life easier while continuing her destructive lifestyle.

Is there a lesson for us? Yes, a lesson about the stories all of us live. The conversation between Jesus and the woman reveals two things about our stories. First, our stories are complex and multi-layered. Think of hers.

She was a minority, a Samaritan in a predominately Jewish part of the world. She was a woman in a man's culture and was completely dependent upon the provisions of men. She had to live – she had to come to the well to draw water and was despised by others for she had slept with at least six men in the village. Every day she endured the shame as it penetrated to the depths of her soul. She probably was never invited over for a party, a baby shower, or a lady's tea. She was isolated, and all these issues wound their way into her heart in complex, layered patterns that made life confusing. Does this sound familiar for someone you know? Does it sound familiar for you?

> The conversation between Jesus and the woman reveals two things about our stories. First, our stories are complex and multi-layered. Second, in spite of the many layers and complexities, we find it easy to focus on the surface needs and will do everything we can to avoid the destructive layers underneath.

The conversation between Jesus and the woman reveals a second truth about the stories we live. In spite of the many layers and complexities of our stories, we find it easy to focus on the surface needs and will do everything we can to avoid the destructive layers underneath. Those are the untouchables. Those are the areas we wish to leave unvisited, and those are the areas that give us the greatest pain.

When the woman said, "give me this water," was she really asking for spiritual water, for a relationship with the living God? How much did she want this, and how much did she want her immediate, physical, felt needs met?

Isn't that the way it is with us? We have surface needs like food and water, jobs and a place to live, where to put the kids in school. And we also have deep Issues like shame, the pain of prejudice, and loneliness, but we are reluctant to bring these issues up and we continue to focus on the surface, felt needs – what will help us survive today.

We can fool people and hide from them, but can we ever hide them from the Lord? This woman was soon to learn that she could not hide anything from Jesus. He was not fooled, and he moved beyond her immediate need of water, beyond the deeper needs of being a woman in a man's world and being a Samaritan in a Jewish culture. He went for the deepest need in her life.

Jesus said, "Go, call your husband and come back" knowing that the man she is living with is not her husband and she is in sin.

The woman tries to sidestep the issue and she tells Jesus a half truth. "I have no husband."

For a moment, Jesus, plays her game and says, "You are right. You have no husband."

The woman breathes a sigh of relief knowing that she escaped this man who is making her very uncomfortable, but this relief is short-lived because Jesus moves in for the kill.

"Woman, you have had five husbands and the man you are sleeping with now isn't your husband."

We really need to be honest with God, don't we? Why are we not honest with God? Why do we work so hard at sidestepping him or avoiding him or changing the subject? Shame, fear of rejection, too much pain, fear that if we are honest he is going to ask us to do something we can't afford to do or don't want to do. I'm sure we could all come up with a list of reasons why we try to avoid him.

Until we are honest with God we are not going to identify our greatest needs and we are going to continue to focus on getting water. We are going to continue to focus on convenient surface things while our greatest needs go unmet.

What were her greatest needs?

How about – the need to be cherished? She had married and divorced five times. She had been used and discarded .. used and discarded … used and discarded … used and discarded … used and discarded.

How does that make one feel? Like a piece of trash, like a physical object for a man's pleasure rather than a whole person who has much to offer and who longs for a relationship? What does that do to a person over time when they are treated this way?

Now, in spite of the way she had been treated, she is with another man and this time didn't even bother with a ceremony. They were just living together. Apparently she had lost hope of ever having any kind of happiness.

She was numb to life.

The fountainhead of her life, those deepest areas that were made for joy were blocked by the pain of her life experiences. Jesus wanted to send the rushing rivers of his living water to this place in her thirsty soul to unblock the dam that was slowly robbing her of life.

> Until we are honest with God we are not going to identify our greatest needs and we are going to continue to focus on getting water. We are going to continue to focus on convenient surface things while our greatest needs go unmet.

One would think at this point in the story the woman would fall on her face, weeping, and say, "you are right. I am a sinner, and I have had so many problems and disappointments. Please have mercy on me and help me."

While that happens with some people, it doesn't happen with others because some people are just tough cases, and as we said, people's stories and their pain is complex and multi-layered. This woman was one of these complex, multi-layered, tough cases, and she said,

"Sir, I can see that you are a prophet. Our fathers worshiped on this mountain, Mt. Gerizim, but you Jews claim that the place where we must worship is in Jerusalem."

What? The woman has just had her heart exposed, the deepest needs of her life revealed, and she tries to sidestep them with a theological question?

The Samaritans believed the place to worship was on Mt. Gerizim. They believed in the first five books of the Law of Moses and in those books there is a statement that God's people were to build an altar to the Lord on Mt. Gerizim near the city of Shechem in the area that became known as Samaria. This is where this woman lived and where the Samaritans worshiped.

Religious and cultural hatred intensified between the Jews and Samaritans. Back and forth it went for centuries. Who was right? How could one follow God with certainty? How could she follow God with certainty? How could she make her life right with God when there were so many different ideas about how to approach him?

If she did discover the truth, would God even accept her?

And so she asks, "Sir, I see that you are a prophet." – for who but a prophet could see into her life with such clarity and reveal her sin – "Sir, I see that you are a prophet, so please tell me who is right? Is it our Samaritan fathers who have held fast to the Law of Moses and say that we must worship on Mt. Gerizim or is it you Jews who say we must worship in Jerusalem? Even if I wanted to get my life right with God, I wouldn't know where to go."

What would you say to her? What kind of answer would you give? When Jesus replied to her, he gave an answer that would set her free and set all others free who face such religious and cultural dilemmas.

"Believe me, woman, a time is coming when you will worship the Father neither on this mountain nor in Jerusalem. There has been a long-standing dispute between Samaritans and Jews. You have been worshiping what you do not know. We Jews have been worshiping what we know for salvation for the world comes from the Jews. Yet a time is coming and has even now dawned in the world when these mountains will no longer be important, for the true worshipers will worship the Father in spirit and truth. They are the kind of worshipers the Father seeks. God is spirit, and his worshipers must worship in spirit and in truth."

Let's break down what Jesus said.

First, Jesus broke through the long-standing religious barrier that stated that the primary worship of God must be in one place – Jerusalem. For a season in the history of God's people this was important to protect the people from idolatry. Mt. Gerizim was not the place that God originally designed for his people to worship. Before worship could go worldwide, God designated one city where his worship and where sacrifices would be offered – Jerusalem – not Mt. Gerizim. Salvation came from the Jewish people and not from the Samaritans. And this does show us that while Jesus' goal was to make the worship of God a worldwide experience for all people, all people still needed to know that there were wrong ways of approaching God and right ways of approaching him. The Samaritans had it wrong and needed to change some things.

Jesus did correct the woman, but Jesus did not dwell on this for he quickly refocused on the goal of getting to the woman's heart. Jesus declared that the season of worshiping in Jerusalem exclusively was now over, and the time had come when it no longer mattered what city one worshipped in. That's comforting to know in this day when his followers live around the globe, to know that the worship of the true God can take place anywhere!

Second, Jesus shows that worship consists of two elements. It consists of truth and spirit. People need to embrace both. The Jews did have the truth. The Samaritans did not. But the Jews did not have the right spirit. They did not need to hate the Samaritan people. God was looking for people who had both truth and spirit. God was looking for people who were committed to the truth of his word but who also worshipped with the right heart – the right spirit.

Third, it teaches us what God really wants. He wants our heart and our worship. As Jesus said, "Such people the Father seeks to be *his worshippers*." The world was full of lies and hatred, animosity between peoples such as the Samaritans and Jews, and false ideas like the ones the Samaritans had. But the time had come to correct all errors of the mind with the truth and to heal the hatred of the spirit with the forgiveness and the love of God. Such is the desire of God today as he seeks for people who will worship him in spirit and in truth.

~~~

The conversation between Jesus and the woman of Sychar has plunged into deep waters. He has put His finger on her deepest need and he has solved a perplexing religious issue of her day. What would she say to him? What would she do?

The woman of Sychar who came to the well was a thirsty woman, but the thirst of her soul far exceeded the thirst of her body and she was learning that the man with whom she spoke might have what she had longed for all her life.

How about you? Are you thirsty? Why not drink from the water that Jesus offers. Why not enter into a conversation with Him, tell Him all your problems and let Him bring healing, forgiveness, and life to your deepest needs.

Read the Story as Originally Told in John 4:1-24

[1] Therefore when the Lord knew that the Pharisees had heard that Jesus was making and baptizing more disciples than John [2] (although Jesus Himself was not baptizing, but His disciples were), [3] He left Judea and went away again into Galilee. [4] And He had to pass through Samaria. [5] So He came to a city of Samaria called Sychar, near the parcel of ground that Jacob gave to his son Joseph; [6] and Jacob's well was there. So Jesus, being wearied from His journey, was sitting thus by the well. It was about the sixth hour.

[7] There came a woman of Samaria to draw water. Jesus said to her, "Give Me a drink." [8] For His disciples had gone away into the city to buy food. [9] Therefore the Samaritan woman said to Him, "How is it that You, being a Jew, ask me for a drink since I am a Samaritan woman?" (For Jews have no dealings with Samaritans.) [10] Jesus answered and said to her, "If you knew the gift of God, and who it is who says to you, 'Give Me a drink,' you would have asked Him, and He would have given you living water." [11] She said to Him, "Sir, You have nothing to draw with and the well is deep; where then do You get that living water? [12] You are not greater than our father Jacob, are You, who gave us the well, and drank of it himself and his sons and his cattle?" [13] Jesus answered and said

to her, "Everyone who drinks of this water will thirst again; [14] but whoever drinks of the water that I will give him shall never thirst; but the water that I will give him will become in him a well of water springing up to eternal life."

[15] The woman said to Him, "Sir, give me this water, so I will not be thirsty nor come all the way here to draw." [16] He said to her, "Go, call your husband and come here." [17] The woman answered and said, "I have no husband." Jesus said to her, "You have correctly said, 'I have no husband'; [18] for you have had five husbands, and the one whom you now have is not your husband; this you have said truly." [19] The woman said to Him, "Sir, I perceive that You are a prophet. [20] Our fathers worshiped in this mountain, and you people say that in Jerusalem is the place where men ought to worship." [21] Jesus said to her, "Woman, believe Me, an hour is coming when neither in this mountain nor in Jerusalem will you worship the Father. [22] You worship what you do not know; we worship what we know, for salvation is from the Jews. [23] But an hour is coming, and now is, when the true worshipers will worship the Father in spirit and truth; for such people the Father seeks to be His worshipers. [24] God is spirit, and those who worship Him must worship in spirit and truth."

Cultural and Historical Insights

➤ A Jewish ruling in the first century said that "the daughters of the Samaritans are menstruants from their cradle," and therefore always unclean.
➤ The exact origin of the Samaritans is not conclusively known, but what many think today is that they most likely were a

remnant of Jews from the northern kingdom of Israel who had survived the Assyrian conquest in 722 BC. Many centuries later, when Ezra and Nehemiah were enacting their reforms in the little kingdom of Judah to the south, some of the Jewish priests were expelled from the Temple and made their way north to where these people lived. They eventually built a rival temple to the one in Jerusalem and through the centuries developed the conviction that the Temple in Jerusalem was led by a group of wicked priests and that their practices at their Temple on Mt. Gerizim were pure before God.

➢ In 128 BC a group of Jewish warriors attacked the Samaritans and destroyed the temple on Mt. Gerizim. In the year, AD 6 or 7, a group of Samaritan men dressed up like Jewish priests, hid bones of dead people in their garments, went into the Jewish temple in Jerusalem and scattered them about the Temple grounds to defile their sacred place of worship. One wonders if they laughed at this prank all the way back to Samaria! But it was much more than a prank, to a Jew no greater insult could be leveled than to desecrate the holy temple of God.

➢ Living water was water that came directly from God, as in rainwater. It had not been touched by man. Sychar had no streams or lakes in its vicinity and the offer of living water from Jesus would have been a claim of special power from God. Living water was used in ritual baths to make people clean before God.

This information is from the article, "Samaritans," in the *Dictionary of Jesus and the Gospels*, IVP, 724-728.

Reflection

The woman of Sychar lived in a man's world and was a Samaritan in a part of the world predominantly Jewish. How did this affect the way she thought about herself? How do you feel as a woman in today's world? Do you feel valued? Oppressed?

_____

_____

_____

The woman of Sychar had five husbands and was living with a sixth man. Why do you think she had not bothered to marry the sixth man? How do you think she felt having been with so many men in her life? Do you think she was happy or full of turmoil?

_____

_____

_____

What do you think her greatest needs were?

_____

_____

_____

Jesus said God was looking for people who would worship Him in spirit and in truth. What does it mean to worship God in spirit?

_____

_____

_____

What does it mean to worship God in truth?

_____

_____

_____

Are you a worshipper of the true God in spirit and in truth?

_____

_____

_____

Listen to this story online at http://wgsministries.org/stories/ministry/. Click on **Voices in the Wilderness** *(SM001-010)*, scroll down to **The Thirsty Woman Part 1 – SM008**, and play.

Jonathan Williams

The Thirsty Woman – Part 2

Hope has awakened in the heart of the thirsty woman. She hurries back to the village to tell the men about her conversation with Jesus. But what will their response be? Will they listen to her story and believe her remarkable tale?

5 THE THIRSTY WOMAN – PART 2

Jesus, a Jewish man, and an unnamed woman from Samaria have engaged in a conversation about water. The woman came to the well to get water for her household needs. Jesus came to the well to speak to her about the living water that would meet her heart's deepest needs.

The woman asked Jesus for his living water, but Jesus was not so quick to answer her request. She still did not grasp all that he was talking about and so he asked her to do something quite uncomfortable. He asked her to go and bring her husband to him.

"I have no husband," she told him.

But Jesus was not fooled. She had had five husbands and was now living with a sixth man to whom she was not married and when Jesus put his finger on this area of sin and pain, she sidestepped him with a religious question about where people ought to worship. Should she worship on Mt. Gerizim where her people said they should go, or should she worship in Jerusalem where the Jews said people should go?

Even if she wanted to get her life right, she wouldn't be sure where to go or what to do. This is when Jesus spoke to her about the greater reality coming into the world that would solve her problems and the problems of all the people of the earth.

God was spirit – not an image made by man. God could not be located and limited to one place. God was looking for people who would worship him in spirit and in truth.

Let's listen to these amazing words of Jesus again:

"Believe me, woman, a time is coming when you will worship the Father neither on this mountain nor in Jerusalem. There has been a long-standing dispute between Samaritans and Jews. You have been worshiping what you do not know. We Jews have been worshiping what we know for salvation for the world comes from the Jews. Yet a time is coming and has even now dawned in the world when these mountains will no longer be important, for the true worshipers will worship the Father in spirit and truth. They are the kind of worshipers the Father seeks. God is spirit, and his worshipers must worship in spirit and in truth."

When Jesus finished these words, the woman said to Him - "I know that Messiah is coming. When he comes, he will explain everything to us."

The Samaritans believed a Messiah-like figure would come and bring the truth to them. They called him "The Prophet" based upon the words of Moses in Deuteronomy 18:15-18 that God would raise up another prophet like him who would speak God's message to the people. This is the one she was referring to when she said, "I know that Messiah is coming. When he comes, he will explain everything to us."

But I find it astounding that the woman would say this to Jesus!

Had he not just revealed her deepest secrets? Had he not just made her religious issue of no consequence when he told her that the Gerizim/Jerusalem debate was outdated because God was looking upon the heart of people and not the place of worship?

She still holds him at arms-length even though Jesus had broken down so many barriers to get close to her true heart.

Was there a gender problem – a male/female issue? Jesus broke it down by talking with her respectfully, he a man talking with a woman.

Was there a cultural problem – a Samaritan/Jewish issue? Jesus, a Jewish man broke it down by speaking with her, a Samaritan woman about Gerizim and Jerusalem without cultural animosity.

Was there a religious problem – the Samaritan/Jewish debate on the proper place to worship? Jesus solved this issue by pointing to the deeper reality of what God was truly after.

Was there a sin problem – marriage to five men/ living with her sixth man? Jesus broke through this issue by pinpointing the problem, yet without condemnation.

What more could she ask of him, yet she tried to brush him off one last time by saying, "I know Messiah is coming. When he comes, he will explain everything to us."

But because Jesus loved her so much, he would not be brushed off and so he said, "I who speak to you am he."

There it was, finally. Everything in the conversation had pointed to this moment when Jesus would reveal who he really was – he was the Messiah. He was the one Jews and Samaritans … and the whole world were looking for. She knew he was no ordinary man. She had asked early in the conversation if he were greater than the patriarch Jacob, and he was. She had told him later in their conversation that she perceived he was a prophet, and he was that, too. But he was greater. He was the promised one. He was the one all Jews and all Samaritans and all people of the world looked for. And when he identified himself as the promised one, she set down her water pot and without a word ran back to the village.

As she ran, she noticed that same group of Jewish men who had been in the village buying food. They were now leaving the village with arms full of supplies and making their way to the very same well where Jesus was. Who were those men? It didn't matter. She had others to whom she must talk. She ran breathlessly into the village and gathered all the men she knew to tell them about Jesus.

You will notice in the story that she went to the men. She wasn't on good speaking terms with the women but was very familiar with the men in the village and could speak to them. "You need to come and see a man who told me everything that I have done!"

"Slow down, woman. Let's start from the beginning. Who are you talking about?" And when she told them that she had been conversing with a Jewish man at the village well they said, "A Jewish man? You know we have nothing to do with the Jewish people."

"Yes, I know," she said, "but this man told me everything. I was there to draw water and he offered me a different kind of water,

water that cleanses the heart of sin and that if anyone drinks from it he will never thirst again."

The men listened – their hearts were thirsty too. "Go on," they said.

"Then, he talked to me about my sin. Somehow he knew that I had been married to you, and to you, and to you, and to you, and to you. And he knew that I was living with you – right now!" The men squirmed and became a little pale as she pointed to each of them. They knew they were at fault as much as she.

"How much did you tell him," they demanded.

"Tell him? I didn't reveal anything. He knew it all, already. He is a prophet, and then when I asked him about our temple on Gerizim and the temple in Jerusalem he had the most wonderful answer. He said a time was coming and had even now started in the world where it didn't matter where people worshiped. He explained that God is spirit and he cannot be confined to one place. God is not looking at the outward place. He is looking at the heart, and he wants people to worship in spirit and truth. When I told him that Messiah would bring all of the truth to us he said, 'I am the Messiah.' This is not the Messiah is it? You have to come and see."

And so the men left the village and followed the thirsty woman to the village well.

In the meantime, Jesus' disciples had returned. They saw that he was speaking with a Samaritan woman and were quite amazed that he was doing so. They had seen him talk to many men, but not to women. And they had seen him talk to other Jewish men, but to a Samaritan woman? They had a lot to learn about Jesus, but they dismissed it and started getting ready for the meal.

Finally when everything was ready and when one of them blessed the food, the disciples hungrily started devouring what was before them, but Jesus made no move toward the food.

"Teacher, eat," they said.

"I have food to eat that you do not know about."

The disciples looked at one another and said, "What's he talking about? Did someone bring him food? Did that woman give him something to eat? But where would she get food?"

Jesus watched and listened for a few moments. Like the woman at the well, they were missing the point. She was focused on physical water. They were focused on physical food.

Finally, Jesus said, "My nourishment comes from doing the will of God who sent me and from finishing his work. You know the saying, 'Four months between planting and harvest.' But I say, wake up and look around. The fields are already ripe for harvest. The harvesters are paid good wages, and the fruit they harvest is people brought to eternal life. What joy awaits both the planter and the harvester alike! Here is another saying, 'One plants and another harvests.' I sent you to harvest where you didn't plant; others have already done the work, and now you will get to gather the harvest."

Just as Jesus had to explain to the woman about living water and true worship, even so he had to explain to his disciples about true work and satisfying food. True work was not a day's activity to earn a wage to buy food. True work was that which advanced the purposes of God in the world for people who needed him. True food was not what went into the belly to nourish the body but it was that which went into the heart of man to nourish one's soul.

Let's take a closer look at what Jesus said. First, the most important nourishment man needs is not physical food. One wonders if, when Jesus said these words, he was remembering his encounter in the wilderness with the tempter. The tempter had wanted him to satisfy his hunger by turning stones into bread but Jesus said, "Man shall not live by bread alone but by every word that comes from the mouth of God."

What was coming from the mouth of God at this moment? It was a message of life for an entire village in Samaria – women and men desperately hungry and desperately thirsty. God's will was for Jesus to focus on their needs rather than lunch. He could eat later. For the moment his focus was on doing the will of God. His priority was to accomplish the work of God. It was obvious God was at work in the heart of this thirsty woman of Samaria. He was also at work in the hearts of the thirsty men. If that is what God was doing, then Jesus would be right there working with him.

> Just as Jesus had to explain to the woman about living water and true worship even so he had to explain to his disciples about true work and satisfying food. True work was not a day's activity to earn a wage . True work advanced the purposes of God for people who needed him. True food was that which went into the heart of man to nourish one's soul.

What a lesson for us! It is so easy to get focused on daily needs – our food, especially, and miss what God may be doing around us that may require us to skip a meal or to delay some other physical gratification. Oh, for hearts that are sensitive to the work of God around us!

Second, Jesus changed the metaphor. He went from speaking of the work of God as a meal to the work of God as a harvest. This was something the people of God were accustomed to hearing. The prophets had long ago spoken of a great harvest.

> You shall multiply the nation, you shall increase their gladness. They will be glad in your presence as with the gladness of harvest, as men rejoice when they divide the spoil. – Isaiah 9:3

> "Israel was holy to the Lord, the first of his harvest. All who ate of it became guilty. Evil came upon them," declares the Lord." – Jeremiah 2:3

> Also, O Judah, there is a harvest appointed for you, When I restore the fortunes of my people. – Hosea 6:11

Jesus was saying that this promised time of harvest was upon them. He said, "You plant your seed and then you say harvest will come in four months. That's the way God has ordered his physical world. But in the spiritual world things can happen much faster! Lift up your eyes and see the fields. They are ready for the harvest now. The harvest is ready to be reaped."

One wonders if the men of the village who had started their walk to the village well were now visible to him and the disciples. He had planted one seed in the heart of one woman just a few minutes before and now that seed had already grown up and was bearing a harvest of souls. The fields were indeed ready for harvesting.

Jesus added a third image to explain what was happening to his disciples – wages. When farmers work their fields, they do so that they might reap the crop, or, if they are hired help, they do so that they might receive a wage for their day's work. When all the work is done, the farmer who planted the seed and the workers who reaped from that planting rejoice together. One sows and another reaps. But they all benefit.

Jesus had sown the seed of the kingdom in the heart of the woman. A great harvest was about to be reaped in the village and Jesus was calling his men to join with him in this great harvest. Yes, it was time to eat but a better, more satisfying meal was walking down the road toward them. Not a meal of meat and bread but a meal of satisfying the needs of human hearts. This harvest was not a harvest of wheat or barley but a gathering of men's hearts for life eternal.

Jesus ended these lessons with these words, "What joy awaits both the planter and the harvester alike! You know the saying, 'One plants and another harvests.' And it's true. I sent you to harvest where you didn't plant; others have already done the work, and now you get to gather the harvest." Jesus was talking about his work with the woman that would lead to his work with the men in the village. Jesus was inviting his disciples to join him in this big job that was about to begin with these village men.

I find this to be comforting, challenging, and exciting as we think that Jesus is at work in the hearts of people all around us at this moment. He invites us to open our eyes, to look upon the harvest and to work with him to bring in this great harvest.

~~~

When the Samaritan men came to the well, they met Jesus and his followers. What a strange sight that must have been to others who were passing by at that moment. Think of it. Here was a group of Jewish and Samaritan men talking freely to one another and seeming to enjoy it – like a family talking around a camp fire at night. This is not a random isolated conversation between one Jewish man and one Samaritan that probably happened from time to time as people interacted with each other out of necessity. This was a group of Jewish and Samaritan men conversing without animosity at the village well!

What did they say? What did the men ask Jesus? What did Jesus tell them? We don't know, but what we do know is what it led to. The Samaritan men were intrigued enough by this Jewish teacher that they invited him and his disciples into their homes! They were offering Middle Eastern hospitality where they would seek to meet every need of their guests in an honorable way.

Jesus and his disciples picked up their belongings and the food they had prepared and walked with the Samaritan men to their village and into their homes and stayed two days. These men had Jesus all to themselves and one wonders how the entire village was affected as others saw this unusual and strange sight of Jewish and Samaritan men enjoying each other and learning to love one another. One wonders how many others were touched by Christ in those two days. We know these men to whom the woman first spoke had their lives changed for the story tells us that they believed in Him. And it all started because of a conversation between Jesus and a thirsty woman.

Perhaps we can discover an idea of what Jesus said to these men.

He talked about their hearts. Jesus revealed to the woman the depth of her sin, the things that she thought no one else could know. In the same way, he spoke to them about the depths of their hearts. But they were not afraid for they learned that he would do this with compassion, not condemnation.

Have you let Jesus talk to you about the depths of your heart? Don't be afraid. Tell him everything. He knows it all anyway, but he wants you to be open and honest with him and here is the good news – he will not condemn you.

This is what those men were experiencing – revelation of sin without wrath for their hearts were humble and God's heart was full of love.

He talked about living water. This is what started the conversation in the first place with the woman. He asked her for a drink of water as a prelude to his offer of living water. As they drank water from the well during their many meals together over the next two days, water from the woman's pitcher that eventually got filled, they must have thought about his living water. As the water from the well would pass through their throats and satisfy their thirst, they found the living water of Jesus' words going deep into their souls and quenching the deeper spiritual thirst they had suffered for years.

He talked about the nature of God. They had never heard any man speak like this. Because God was spirit, and not flesh, he was better served by the hearts of people who were humble before him rather than by temples made with hands, whether they were temples in Gerizim or Jerusalem. Yes, it was true that Jerusalem was the place God had appointed for his people but that was just a prelude to what he really wanted – a worldwide family who would worship him anywhere and everywhere Jew, Samaritan, and gentile would gather. The Father was seeking for people who would worship in spirit and in truth.

The two days were now ended. It was time for Jesus to move on. He and his disciples said their goodbyes and started on their way to Galilee escorted by the men to the village boundaries. When Jesus and his disciples were out of sight, the men turned to the woman who had first talked with Jesus and said, "We first believed because of your word and we thank you for telling us about him. But now, after these two days and after hearing him ourselves we believe that he is indeed the Savior of Jew and Samaritan, male and female. Indeed, he is the Savior of the whole world!"

The woman reflected on the amazing events of the past few days. It all started with her thirst, and her familiar journey to the village well, and then, a conversation with Jesus.

~~~

A conversation with Jesus can be life-changing. Have you had that conversation with him? Have you let him talk to you about the deepest needs in your heart?

He is the giver of the water of life that will spring up within you to eternal life. Have you drunk from his well? Have you tasted his water? Why not open your heart to him and let him satisfy your weary soul with his life giving water. Then, when you have tasted, go and tell another of what he has done for you. Like the thirsty woman, perhaps God will use you to lead a group of others to him and they too can hear his life-satisfying words.

Read the Story as Originally Told in John 4:10-45

[10] *Jesus answered and said to her, "If you knew the gift of God, and who it is who says to you, 'Give Me a drink,' you would have asked Him, and He would have given you living water."* [11] *She said to Him, "Sir, You have nothing to draw with and the well is deep; where then do You get that living water?* [12] *You are not greater than our father Jacob, are You, who gave us the well, and drank of it himself and his sons and his cattle?"* [13] *Jesus answered and said to her, "Everyone who drinks of this water will thirst again;* [14] *but whoever drinks of the water that I will give him shall never thirst; but the water that I will give him will become in him a well of water springing up to eternal life."* [15] *The woman said to Him, "Sir, give me this water, so I will not be thirsty nor come all the way here to draw."* [16] *He said to her, "Go, call your husband and come here."* [17] *The woman answered and said, "I have no husband." Jesus said to her, "You have correctly said, 'I have no husband';* [18] *for you have had five husbands, and the one whom you now have is not your husband; this you have said truly."* [19] *The woman said to Him, "Sir, I perceive that You are a prophet.* [20] *Our fathers worshiped in this mountain, and you people say that in Jerusalem is the place where men ought to worship."* [21] *Jesus said to her, "Woman, believe Me, an hour is coming when neither in this mountain nor in Jerusalem will you worship the Father.* [22] *You worship what you do not know; we worship what we know, for salvation is from the Jews.* [23] *But an hour is coming, and now is, when the true worshipers will worship the Father in spirit and truth; for such people the Father seeks to be His worshipers.* [24] *God is spirit, and those who worship Him must worship in spirit and*

truth. *25 The woman said to Him, "I know that Messiah is coming (He who is called Christ); when that One comes, He will declare all things to us." 26 Jesus said to her, "I who speak to you am He."*

27 At this point His disciples came, and they were amazed that He had been speaking with a woman, yet no one said, "What do You seek?" or, "Why do You speak with her?" 28 So the woman left her waterpot, and went into the city and said to the men, 29 "Come, see a man who told me all the things that I have done; this is not the Christ, is it?" 30 They went out of the city, and were coming to Him.

31 Meanwhile the disciples were urging Him, saying, "Rabbi, eat." 32 But He said to them, "I have food to eat that you do not know about." 33 So the disciples were saying to one another, "No one brought Him anything to eat, did he?" 34 Jesus said to them, "My food is to do the will of Him who sent Me and to accomplish His work. 35 Do you not say, 'There are yet four months, and then comes the harvest'? Behold, I say to you, lift up your eyes and look on the fields, that they are white for harvest. 36 Already he who reaps is receiving wages and is gathering fruit for life eternal; so that he who sows and he who reaps may rejoice together. 37 For in this case the saying is true, 'One sows and another reaps.' 38 I sent you to reap that for which you have not labored; others have labored and you have entered into their labor."

39 From that city many of the Samaritans believed in Him because of the word of the woman who testified, "He told me all the things that I have done." 40 So when the Samaritans came to Jesus, they were asking Him to stay with them; and He stayed there two days. 41 Many more believed because of His word; 42 and they were saying to the woman, "It is no longer because of what you said that we believe, for we have heard for ourselves and know that this One is indeed the Savior of the world."

[43] *After the two days He went forth from there into Galilee.* [44] *For Jesus Himself testified that a prophet has no honor in his own country.* [45] *So when He came to Galilee, the Galileans received Him, having seen all the things that He did in Jerusalem at the feast; for they themselves also went to the feast.*

Cultural and Historical Insights

➢ During the time of Alexander the Great, a great uprising against Greek culture occurred in Samaria, but this was severely repressed and a group of Samaritans went from the city of Samaria to Shechem to settle. These may have also been joined by a group of priests from Jerusalem who had previously left Ezra and Nehemiah and who claimed to be the true priesthood of Israel.

➢ They built a temple on Mt. Gerizim and believed that the Books of Moses ordered them to sacrifice to the Lord on Gerizim. The passage is in Deuteronomy 27.

➢ Samaritans believed in one God, in Moses, in the Law, in the place of sacrifice on Mt. Gerizim, and the return of a prophet or a *Taheb* – a restorer.

➢ In 128 BC John Hyrcanus, the leader of the Jewish nation in Judah, captured Shechem and destroyed the temple. This caused the Samaritans to become even more focused in their beliefs that they were following God in the right way and created much more animosity between them and the Jewish people.

> Between AD 6 and 7 some Samaritans littered the Temple in Jerusalem with bones. This would cause ritual impurity for the Jews and they would have to cleanse the entire Temple from this defilement.
> In AD 52 Samaritans massacred Galilean pilgrims on their way to Jerusalem.
> Samaritans believed this prophet would be like Moses. A man by the name of Dositheus claimed to be this prophet. Another prophet-like figure in AD 36 claimed that he would reveal sacred vessels hidden by Moses and he assembled a crowd on Mt. Gerizim. He then, disappeared when his claims did not prove true.

This information is from the article, "Samaritans," in the *Dictionary of Jesus and the Gospels*, IVP, 724-728.

Reflection

When the woman left her water pot at the well and ran into the village to talk with the men about her conversation with Jesus, what do you think she said to them?

_____

_____

_____

Rather than eat the food the disciples had bought and prepared, Jesus said he had other food to eat. How would you describe this kind of food? Have you ever had a time in your life when doing God's will was more satisfying than food?

_____

_____

_____

Jesus talked about people sowing, reaping and rejoicing together. Do you have relationships with others where some may be sowing and some may be reaping, but all are working toward the same goal of reaping a spiritual harvest?

_____

_____

_____

Jesus said a spiritual harvest could come a lot quicker than a physical harvest. Have you been planting seed in the spiritual world and have you been reaping a spiritual harvest in your life or in the lives of others?

_____

_____

_____

Listen to this story online at http://wgsministries.org/stories/ministry/. Click on **Voices in the Wilderness *(SM001-010)*,** scroll down to **The Thirsty Woman Part 2 – SM009,** and play.

Jonathan Williams

Calamities
in the Kitchen

It is a grand day! Jesus has come to the
home of Martha, Mary, and their brother,
Lazarus. Martha is excited to do her best
for this great man but when things go
wrong in the kitchen she loses her
composure and learns an important lesson
about what matters most.

6 CALAMITIES IN THE KITCHEN

Jesus told a story about a man left for dead, the story we commonly call The Good Samaritan, and when he told it, he may have been very close to that very same road in the story, the difficult road connecting Jerusalem and Jericho. The road from Jerusalem to Jericho was 17 miles and a notorious site for robbers which is why people usually traveled in groups. When Jesus finished telling this great story that has so profoundly impacted the world, he started walking up the road toward Jerusalem. He had been there only weeks before. He had stated many things about himself that all needed to hear – he was the light of the world, he was the giver of the water of life, he was the door to life, he was the good shepherd.

In his story about the man left for dead, he turned the world upside down by making a hated Samaritan the hero of his story and by telling all people that the real question in life was not who was their neighbor, but who were they a neighbor to.

The story was now finished and Jesus and his men trudged up the long pathway ascending over 3600 feet in those miles. Their destination, however, was not Jerusalem. The place Jesus had in mind was Bethany, a small village 1½ to 2 miles east of Jerusalem. Here Jesus would stay with his disciples and would have an encounter with two sisters that would never be forgotten.

Bethany was an important town in Israel. According to the Temple Scroll, one of the documents discovered among the Dead Sea Scrolls, the Jews designated three places east of Jerusalem to care for the sick. One of these was Bethany. In their purity rules, the Jews established a perimeter around Jerusalem saying that nothing unclean should come within that boundary. Jerusalem, above all, must remain a holy city. But the sick did need to be cared for and Bethany was an ideal location for it was close to the great city yet outside the perimeter established by the religious leaders. It was to the southeast of the Mount of Olives and could therefore not be seen from anywhere in Jerusalem. Because it was out of sight, it was a suitable place to care for the sick.

Bethany was also a favorite site for pilgrims travelling from the north in Galilee. In order not to come into contact with the hated Samaritans, the Jews would bypass Samaria to the east of the Jordan River, come to Jericho, and then traverse up the steep road and lodge in Bethany, the final stop before coming to Jerusalem.

Hospitality to travelers and care for the sick, Bethany was indeed a special village and in it lived a man and his two sisters. Their names were Lazarus, Martha, and Mary.

When Jesus entered the village, Martha, the older of the two sisters welcomed Jesus. We don't know if Lazarus was there to welcome him. Perhaps he was away on business or perhaps he was not yet a follower of Jesus while his sisters Mary and Martha were. Whichever the case, Martha took it upon herself to greet

Jesus as he entered the village and to invite him to her home where her brother and sister lived, and Jesus accepted her invitation of hospitality.

Hospitality in the ancient world, and in many parts of our world today, was a blessed gift to travelers. Among the Jewish people its virtue was extolled. Hosts would often go out to greet travelers and escort them back to the house.

A faithful Jewish household would eagerly look forward to entertaining people. In Jerusalem, no man was to count his house as his own, and this attitude certainly spilled over to the surrounding villages such as Bethany. During the feasts when the population of Jerusalem would swell, there was room for all. Owners of homes would hang curtains at their front door to show travelers that room was available. This hospitality was especially seen in Bethany.

"Let your house be wide open, and let the poor be the children of your house," went one saying among the people. Some said there should be four doors to every house to welcome guests from every direction.

The rabbis, the teachers of the people, had many things to say about the importance of hospitality. Some said hospitality involved as great a merit as attendance at an academy of learning in Jerusalem. Others said to entertain a wise man and to send him away with presents was as meritorious as the daily sacrifices in the temple.

The receiving and entertainment of strangers was considered as great as receiving the glory of God. One rabbi read Psalm 109:31 – "God shall stand at the right hand of the poor," and said, "Whenever a poor man stands at your door, the Holy One, blessed be his name, stands at his right hand. Give him alms, knowing that you shall receive a reward from him who stands at his right hand."

The rabbis taught that when giving hospitality, they were imitating God who clothed the naked for he clothed Adam and Eve. God also visited the sick for he visited Abraham in the heat of the day. God comforted the mourners for he blessed Isaac after his father Abraham's death, and God buried the dead for he took care of the body of Moses when he died on Mt. Nebo.

Thus, to be hospitable to others was to imitate God himself who cared for people and when serving guests, a host was to look pleased at all times, to wait upon them himself, to promise them little but to give them much. The guests were expected to say, "At what trouble my host has gone, and all for my sake."

On this day when Jesus and his disciples had trudged up the long, weary road from Jericho to Bethany, Martha welcomed them into her home. After the customary greeting when kisses would be exchanged, feet and hands washed, and oil given for anointing, the men would go to one area of the house where they could rest or talk about Scripture while the women would go into another part of the house and prepare a meal.

Martha's heart was filled with joy! Jesus was in her home! She had heard so much about him! His miracles of healing, his teaching on the Scriptures of God's people, and especially his care for the poor and women. Although respect for women in Israel far exceeded that in gentile communities, did she still believe women were not given the respect or love that should be granted them as the daughters of the God of Israel? Perhaps Jesus would speak about that in her home today. Perhaps she could show how valuable she was. She would take special effort and care on this day to show Jesus her hospitality, to make him and his disciples the best meal, and provide a day for them they would not soon forget.

While Jesus went into the common area with the men to talk, Martha went to the cooking area and began to work. She organized her household servants into groups with specific assignments. Some were sent to the market to buy the necessary items for the meal. Others made sure Jesus and his disciples had the greatest of care and were comfortable.

Everything was in motion under Martha's supervision. Martha also knew that her reputation as an honorable woman was dependent upon her ability to manage her household. How she wanted to do the best job possible. But soon, some problems began to emerge. One servant said, "I'm sorry, the market did not have everything we needed. That special spice to make the meal taste just right was not there." Another said, "The vegetables just didn't seem as fresh as we have come to expect. The pickings just weren't that good today." Another servant came in and confessed that she had broken some valuable pottery in the preparations. Another said that one of the fires must have been too hot because some of the food was burned.

Martha could not believe it. Why were all of these things going wrong on this day above all days when Jesus was in her house! She began to become frustrated and upset and thought, "I can't handle this." And then she looked around and realized someone was missing from the kitchen – Mary her sister was not there. Where was Mary?

Martha went into the courtyard and called out, "Mary, Mary,

where are you?" But Mary was not there. Then she asked one of the servants, "Did Mary go with you to the market?" and the servant replied, "No, Mary has not been with me." Then, with some concern Martha asked several other servants and finally one of them sheepishly said, "I know where Mary is. She is with the men. She is sitting at Jesus' feet listening to him teach."

Sitting at Jesus' feet? Sitting in the room with the men? Martha could hardly believe her ears. Not only was this inappropriate, but Mary's place was by her side helping to get everything ready for the men. No wonder things were going wrong! If Mary had been where she was supposed to be, there would not be this chaos!

Martha walked toward the room where the men were seated. As she approached she could hear their voices. Then she heard Mary's voice asking Jesus a question about the kingdom of God. Martha could not believe it. She came to the doorway of the room, and there was Mary sitting at Jesus' feet and listening to everything he was saying to the men.

She tried to get Mary's attention discreetly. She made faces, she made hissing noises, she motioned to get her attention but Mary was completely focused on Jesus. Just at that moment another servant came up behind Martha and said, "I'm sorry to bother you, but your attention is really needed in the kitchen. You won't believe what has happened now."

And then Martha burst into tears and all the men saw her frustration. Martha came forward to Jesus and said, "Oh Jesus, I am so sorry to disturb your gathering with these men. I have been so busy preparing the meal and nothing is going right, and my sister, she is supposed to help me. If she had been with the women, if she had been where she was supposed to have been I would have had everything ready by now." And Martha burst into tears again while Jesus remained silent and Mary continued to sit at his feet.

Finally, Martha said, "Lord, won't you say something? Don't you care? Don't you care that my sister has left me to do all this serving alone?"

And when Jesus said, "Martha, I do care for you," Martha replied, "Then, tell her to help me."

Jesus said, "Martha, Martha, you are worried and bothered about so many things. But only one thing is necessary. And Mary has chosen this one thing. She has chosen the good part. I will not allow it to be taken away from her."

Martha stood there speechless, humbled in the presence of the Jesus.

~~~

The story of Martha and Mary tells us about the danger of distraction. Martha became angry with her sister, but she did not begin that special day that way. She began Jesus's visit with joy. She had welcomed him into their home. She had wanted to do her best for him. All of this was commendable.

We receive our first clue from the story that something had gone wrong when it tells us that Martha was distracted with all her preparations. The word distracted literally means that she allowed her attention to wander. This may imply that she also wanted to hear from the Lord. Women were taught in synagogues. When Jesus preached in villages women were in attendance. Women received healing from him. And Martha probably looked forward to spending time with Jesus and hearing him. But somewhere along the way she became distracted. After a few minutes the preparations took precedence over listening to Jesus and she began to focus more on things than the Lord. The Greek word used in the text says she was "dragged away with her many services." How interesting that service to the Lord can drag one away from the Lord!

Second, the story tells us that Martha became worried. Jesus said, "Martha, Martha, you are worried about so many things."

The original language gives an interesting picture. The word "worry" originally meant to be pulled in two. At first, Martha was just distracted, there were many things that were vying for her attention and once she began to pay more attention to them, it is as if they sunk their hooks into her and pulled her away from Jesus.

Again, she wanted to hear the Lord, but she wanted to make this a grand occasion for him as well and because she could not be in two places at one time, she did neither well. Distraction grew into the bondage of worry and her heart was pulled apart.

Third, the story tells us that she was bothered. Jesus said, "Martha, Martha you are worried and bothered about so many things."

The word "bothered" literally means "a tumult, a bustle." It refers to agitation like the wind stirring up the waves of the sea. Her mental distraction became emotional worry which showed on her face, in her body movements, and the pace and noise of her service. Don't we all know what that is like? Don't we know the difference between a cupboard door closing and a cupboard door closing a little too hard a few too many times and the pots and pans on the stove clanging more noisily than normal?

Martha's distraction turned into worry which caused her to bustle about the house in her service. She was in a tumult.

Fourth, Martha questioned the Lord's love. Martha went to Jesus and asked, "Lord, do you not care that my sister has left me to do all the serving alone?" I love the first five words of her question, "Lord, do you not care?" One other story in the Gospels uses this exact phrase. When Jesus was in a boat with his disciples a great storm came upon them as Jesus was resting. The disciples were bailing water out but Jesus slept on.

> Martha's solution is an example of how people get trapped into thinking that their problems are because of other people. Martha thought her problems were because of her sister. But Martha's problems were because of Martha.

Finally, some of his disciples came to him at the height of the storm and said, "*Lord, do you not care* that we are perishing?"

Martha used the same words. It's almost as if she is blaming God for her problems. I wonder, if, after she could not get Mary to respond to her attention-getting efforts, she began to look at Jesus with a don't-you-care-about-what-is-happening, don't-you-see-what-is-going-on type of face.

I wonder how many times we have said those things to the Lord or we have felt that way, believing that no one cares or that God doesn't care when we feel like we are sinking.

Martha took one more step in her downward spiral from joy to distress. She became demanding. After Martha asked Jesus if he cared, he probably replied, "Yes, I do care" to which Martha replied, "Then, tell her to help me." Martha thought she had the solution to her problem. Her solution was to drag Mary away from Jesus into her world of problems.

Martha's solution is an example of how people get trapped into thinking that their problems are because of other people. Martha thought her problems were because of her sister. But Martha's problems were because of Martha.

The Lord did care for Martha. He saw what was happening. He saw everything. Though he surely did not want the entire burden to fall on her, there was something far more important than Martha demanding that Mary help her … something far more important that needed to happen in Martha's life.

Jesus said, "only a few things are necessary, really only one and Mary has chosen the good part that will not be taken away from her." What did Martha need? She needed to learn to choose what was best. This story is not teaching us to pursue a life of quiet contemplation in contrast to a life of deeds. The contrast is not a life of devotion verses a life of activity. The issue is choosing what is best in life and what is best in each situation. The issue is continually choosing that which will last forever.

In this story, the best was to sit at Jesus' feet. There was no need for an elaborate meal with all kinds of preparations. Martha did right in welcoming him. Maybe a meal was in order. But these good things became wrong. She lost sight of the priority in her life and in her home … and that priority was listening to Jesus.

Is this not a picture of us? We do good things, we do things we should do, but we lose focus in our work and miss the most important part of life, loving God with all our heart. How interesting that Martha's slide began with being distracted, losing sight of what was most important.

Some of us may need to look at our life and ask, "What am I doing with my life? Am I caught up in endless activities with no purpose and not developing my love relationship with the Lord? Would I characterize my life as distracted or focused on hearing God? Do I have a tendency to worry? Do I get bothered? Do I feel that God doesn't care? Do I blame others and become demanding thinking that I have the solution and if other people would only see things my way then everything would be OK?

> Whatever we are doing, preparing a banquet or reading God's word, we need to enjoy God at that moment, the people he puts into our lives, and the work he has given us as we do what is necessary. When Jesus was extremely busy he was enjoying the company of other people, and enjoying his Father in heaven.

If you answer yes to any of these, you need to look at your life and ask God to show you what is really important.

It is possible to be busy and to be in the center of God's will. That's why I said this story is not about sitting at Jesus' feet vs. doing things. It's not the amount or type of activity but if we are in the center of God's will that matters and our hearts are at rest. Jesus was so busy at times in his life that he did not even have time for a meal. The difference between him and Martha is that he was obeying. God calls us to obedience, not busy-ness. Martha's problem is not that she was busy but that she was busy with the wrong things. Mary was busy too – sitting at the Lord's feet.

All of this teaches us that whatever we are doing, preparing a banquet or reading God's word, we need to enjoy God at that moment, the people he puts into our lives, and the work he has given us as we do what is necessary. When Jesus was extremely busy he was enjoying the company of other people, and enjoying his Father in heaven. If we are not enjoying God that should be a caution that we need to take a break as soon as we can and get focused on what is most important.

It was quite possible Martha could have listened to the Lord for a while, then quietly got up and made a few preparations with a calm heart and mind. She could have gone into the kitchen and prayed, "Lord God of Israel, I would really like to be in there for the whole thing, but I know that you are with me, and as I make these preparations, I make them for you. Lord, I'm glad that Mary can hear what Jesus is saying and I ask that you would bless her. Thank you for her example of devotion to you. And help me to follow that devotion." Then, she could have served the Lord with a sweet spirit, and instead of hearing, "Martha, Martha you are worried and bothered about so much," she could have heard, "Martha, Martha, you have such peace and such sweetness as you go about your duties. You are truly an example of one who worships God with her service."

~~~

Calamity in the kitchen! I think this familiar story is one with which a lot of us can identify. The story is not about people in deep moral sin. It is not about someone who needed to be released from an evil spirit or someone next to death who needed to be raised up. We are talking about people who were doing quite well in life, yet who had normal problems in the home. We are talking about someone who was having a bad day because her self imposed expectations were not being met, and it seemed like nothing was going right. We can all relate to that!

As I was preparing this story, I would often pause and laugh over Martha's silliness and Jesus' patience with her. But as I was laughing at her, I also realized I was laughing at myself because I saw so much of me in her. How about you? Can you identify with her? I ask you today, is your heart at rest with God? What does Jesus say about you?

Read the Story as Originally Told in Luke 10:38-42

[38] Now as they were traveling along, He entered a village; and a woman named Martha welcomed Him into her home. [39] She had a sister called Mary, who was seated at the Lord's feet, listening to His word. [40] But Martha was distracted with all her preparations; and she came up to Him and said, "Lord, do You not care that my sister has left me to do all the serving alone? Then tell her to help me." [41] But the Lord answered and said to her, "Martha, Martha, you are worried and bothered about so many things; [42] but only one thing is necessary, for Mary has chosen the good part, which shall not be taken away from her."

Cultural and Historical Insights

➤ In Jerusalem, no man was to count his house as his own. Households would hang curtains at the front door to show that room was still available.

> During the feasts when the population would swell, there was room for all. And the hospitality was especially seen in Bethphage and Bethany.
> A rabbinic saying – "Let your house be wide open, and let the poor be the children of your house."
> Some said there should be four doors to every house to welcome guests from every direction.
> The rabbis said that hospitality involved as great a merit as attendance at an academy of learning in Jerusalem and that to entertain a wise man and to send him away with presents was as meritorious as the daily sacrifices in the temple and that the receiving and entertainment of strangers was as great as receiving the glory of God.
> Psalm 109:31 – "He shall stand at the right hand of the poor." One rabbi said, "Whenever a poor man stands at your door, the Holy One, blessed be his name, stands at his right hand. Give him alms, knowing that you shall receive a reward from him who stands at his right hand."
> We are told to imitate God who clothed the naked (for he clothed Adam and Eve), who visited the sick (for he visited Abraham in the heat of the day), who comforted the mourners (for he blessed Isaac after his father Abraham's death), and who buried the dead (for he buried Moses.)

> A host is to look pleased when entertaining his guests, to wait upon them himself, to promise them little but to give them much and a guest was expected to say, "At what trouble my host has gone, and all for my sake."

These insights are from Alfred Edersheim, *Sketches of Jewish Social Life,* Hendrickson Publishers, 46-48.

Reflection

Why do you think Martha let so many things distract her? Do you believe this was part of her personality to let this happen? Do distractions keep you from seeking God in your life?

_____

_____

_____

Martha asked the Lord if he cared that all of the burdens of preparing the meal were falling upon her. Have you ever doubted God's care for you? If so, explain the situation and what happened. Did you let God know how you felt?

_____

_____

_____

Jesus said Martha was worried and bothered about so many things. How is your emotional health? Are you worried and bothered by things? If so, list them and pray through each one and give them to the Lord.

_____

_____

_____

How can you follow the example of Mary and focus on the most important things in life?

_____

_____

_____

Listen to this story online at http://wgsministries.org/stories/ministry/. Click on **Conflict in Israel** *(SM031-040)*, scroll down to **Calamities in the Kitchen – SM038**, and play.

The Widow Who Would Not Be Silenced

The disciples are troubled. They have been listening to Jesus speak of the coming judgments and his own death. Fear has settled into their hearts until Jesus tells the story of a courageous widow threatened by the men in her village.

7 THE WIDOW WHO WOULD NOT BE SILENCED

Jesus and his disciples were eating with a group of religious leaders and the disciples were unusually quiet. They seemed concerned and worried. It was not that Pharisees, the religious leaders, were present. Often they caused Jesus problems, testing him, trying to trap him, accusing him unjustly, calling him bad names. No, on this occasion the concern of the disciples was with something Jesus had said.

Earlier in the day the Pharisees had asked Jesus when the kingdom was coming. Jesus replied that the kingdom had already come, not completely, but that the kingdom had been inaugurated in his life and in his ministry. He healed the sick, he gave sight to the blind, he made the lame walk, he cast out evil spirits, and above all, he forgave sinners and renewed their relationship with the living God. He also talked about his death.

Hearing Jesus talk about the power of the kingdom was exciting, but whenever he talked about his death, the disciples didn't understand it. It confused them and they didn't like it. They believed the Messiah should be glorious and live. They believed the Messiah should drive the Romans out of the land. They believed the Messiah should rule the world from Jerusalem. But Jesus kept talking about dying and some kind of resurrection on the third day that would vindicate him. It was all so bewildering.

Jesus also talked about the coming judgment upon his people. He had said not all of the covenant people would be saved. Some would be taken to judgment. He described the judgment like great carrion birds, circling, waiting for the victims to die so they could feed on the flesh, all because of their sin.

The meal continued in silence and gloom settled over them all. Finally, Jesus asked, "Why are your hearts troubled?"

One of the disciples answered, "Lord, when you talk of this judgment upon our people, and when you talk about your suffering, how can we not be troubled? How can we not be saddened with the thought of you being taken away from us and of the coming judgment upon Israel?"

Another disciple said, "Master, it makes me afraid."

Then Jesus said, "let me tell you a story. This will lift your hearts."

~~~

Not far from here lived a woman with her husband and small children. They were both righteous. They feared God and loved their neighbors as they loved themselves. The man owned a small field. He worked it diligently and was able to make enough to provide for his family. But the years took their toll and he was often sick from his long labor in the field.

In the same village was a wealthy landowner. He had much land and many servants. He was also greedy and was always trying to gain more for himself. Many times he tried to obtain the small piece of land the man owned but the man would not sell it. As small as it was, it had been in his family for generations and he aimed to hold it and pass it to his children.

But the greedy landowner kept plotting and scheming to take it away. And then, the unthinkable happened. One evening, the husband did not return home from his field. His wife became worried. She put her small children into the care of a friend and went to the field to search for her husband, and there she found him, dying from the heat, from the exhaustion of the long years of labor, and from worry over the wealthy landowner who had threatened his inheritance.

After the woman buried her husband, it did not take long for the wealthy landowner to approach the woman and begin bargaining with her. He told her how the husband had wanted to sell it to him.

The woman scoffed at him and said, "My husband would never sell this land to anyone, especially to you!"

A few days later the wealthy landowner returned, but this time he tried a different strategy. He said, "I have offered you a price for your land but you will not sell," and the woman quickly replied, "Even if I were to sell, I would not sell it at the price you offer. Your price is a travesty. It is unjust and a mockery before God."

The landowner smiled and continued, ignoring the woman's sharp words. "It has come to my attention, that there are some irregularities in the deed of trust for your land. I will soon go to the judge in our village and tell him of these irregularities if you do not sell to me. You know of him, and you know what he will do when he is, shall I say, properly motivated to make certain decisions. The land will be taken from you and you will lose everything. You and your children will have nothing." Then, he walked away, laughing at her weakness in the world of men.

The woman trembled. She knew of the judge in her village. He was an unrighteous man and was easily bribed. She knew the wealthy landowner could present a formidable legal case against her and that she, a woman, would stand little chance in a court proceeding.

Her fear grew. But as she looked at her children she knew there was only one action to take. She must appear before the judge, and, as wicked as he was, she must cry out to him for legal protection.

The next day, the judge sat in the village gate. He was a large man and dressed luxuriously. He sat upon pillows on his throne and his droopy eyelids, dull with too much wine and food, showed that he was bored with the complaints people brought to him for judgment. The judge was surrounded by his aides. These were also wicked men who took bribes for the judge and decided which cases would be heard. People would line up and call out their requests to be heard, but the judge would ignore them, until one of them would approach his aides and discreetly pass money to them. Then, the judge would have their name called and would hear their case and decide in their favor.

The widow surveyed the situation. It looked impossible. She was a woman. She lived in a world controlled by evil men. She was a widow. In her world, men circled around widows like wolves around a lost lamb. She had little money, and the judge ruled only by bribes and gifts for he did not love justice, had no heart to advance honor, and cared not that his actions were shameful. This man, this judge, did not fear God.

But the woman was undaunted. She laid aside her fears and concerns, and in the presence of the men at the village gates began to cry out to the judge, "Give me legal protection from my opponent! You must hear my case. You must give me legal protection."

The large judge, slightly amused, looked in the direction of the widow, turned to one of his aides and motioned for him to get rid of her. The aide got up, took the woman by the arm, and held out his hand as if he were asking for something, but she angrily walked away. The judge laughed and went back to his business of hearing the cases of those who offered bribes.

But the next day the woman was back. No sooner had the large, sleepy, uncaring judge sat himself upon his cushions than the woman was there screaming at him, "Give me protection from my legal opponent." She would not be quiet. She cried out louder than all the men and again the judge motioned for one of his aides to have her leave.

This went on for some time. Day after day the judge would sit and rule over the people, profiting from their bribes, and day after day the woman would be there shouting to the judge. Nothing could stop her. They couldn't ignore her. They couldn't treat her shamefully in public. Their threats against her had no power, and it seemed they could not outlast her. She was determined to get her way with the judge. She was going to make life miserable for him until he did something.

Finally, one morning, the judge arose after a night of feasting and drinking. He usually arose with great happiness, looking forward to sitting in the place of honor at the village gates and enriching himself from the bribes of people, but on this day, the judge had a headache. "That woman," he said. "That woman is wearing me out. That woman is making me look bad and is making me ill."

He called to one of his aides, "Listen, you know we don't make a ruling unless someone gives us money. You know that I care not for people and that I don't believe in some God and his justice that I am supposed to carry out. But this woman keeps coming to me and crying out. She is making my life miserable. If she comes again today, even if she continues to refuse to give us money, bring her to me, and I will rule in her case."

And so the judge and his aides prepared themselves for the day's work. With great pomp they paraded to the village gates and prepared the platform and the cushions for the throne upon which the judge would sit. As they did this they looked upon the crowd that was forming and in the front of the line was the woman, a look of determination on her face.

The judge sat and the court was announced "in session." And just as the woman started to cry out, "Give me legal protection," one of the aides came up to her and said, "The judge will see you."

The woman was astonished, but she quickly collected her thoughts approached the judge and said, "You know my husband. You know how hard he worked. You know that land is ours. My opponent, the wealthiest landowner in this area is trying to take it from me. This is all I have. You must stop him. You must give me protection."

And the judge leaned close to her and said, "If I do this, does this mean you will stop coming to this place and screaming at me?" And the woman said, "If you give me legal protection, I will never come here again."

The judge breathed a sigh of relief. He turned to one of his aides and gave him some instructions who wrote some things on a parchment, gave it to the woman, and said, "Here is what you have asked for." And the woman, with a look of triumph in her eyes turned and faced the crowd. The men quietly parted and the woman walked through the multitude of men victorious in her quest for justice.

~~~

Jesus looked upon his disciples and said, "Let me now explain this to you. Let me encourage your hearts. The unrighteous judge did it. He granted her request. Listen to what he said. He said that even though he did not fear God or have respect for granting justice to people, he would still do what she asked!"

> "You should be like the woman. Although she feared, she did not let her fear control her. She cried out to the judge every day, and you should cry out to your Father day and night. Even though you are not perfect, he will be very patient with you. He will keep his anger far from you. He will bring about justice for his chosen ones."

"And I say to you, if that *unrighteous* judge gave her justice, don't you think that God in heaven, your Father, who is good and who loves you will bring about justice for his chosen ones? Of course he will. He will keep the covenant with you. He will bring about his covenant righteousness. He will bring his covenant justice to his people.

"You should be like the woman. Although she feared, she did not let her fear control her. She cried out to the judge every day, and you should cry out to your Father day and night. Even though you are not perfect, he will be very patient with you. He will keep his anger far from you. He will bring about justice for his chosen ones.

"I have shared with you that I, the Son of Man, the heavenly one, will be vindicated. Yes, I will suffer but God will vindicate me. I trust in him and he will raise me up. In the same way, you trust in him also. Don't give in to your fear. Have faith in God. I ask, when the Son of Man comes, when the Son of Man is vindicated in the difficult days that will come, will he find you with this kind of faith? Will he find faith on the earth?"

~~~

What a great question Jesus asked his disciples, and it is a question he asks us. As Jesus looks upon the earth today, does he find faith? Let's see how this story applies to our lives.

First, the story reminds us, painfully, that we live in a fallen world. The disciples were fearful. Jesus told the story because the disciples were under stress. Jesus himself was in danger. The disciples were in danger. The political authorities were keeping a wary eye upon Jesus. Herod knew about Jesus and was very concerned that he was causing disturbances in the land. Pilate, the cruel and ruthless Roman governor was also keeping a watchful eye, and he would stop at nothing to keep order. If he determined this movement of people following Jesus was causing problems in the land, he would bring it to a swift end.

The religious rulers were following Jesus and hounding him, trying to trap him with silly questions and discredit him in the eyes of the people. Many of them were plotting to arrest Jesus and kill him, and those who were his closest followers would not be shown mercy either. There was, indeed, much to fear.

If those things were true for those men, how much truer was it for those in society who were vulnerable. Who was more vulnerable than widows and orphans? God, in his Word, set down laws that his leaders should protect them and others who were weak. In Exodus 22:22 we read, "You shall not afflict any widow or orphan. If you afflict him at all, and if he does cry out to Me, I will surely hear his cry." The prophet Isaiah said, "Learn to do good. Seek justice, reprove the ruthless, defend the orphan, plead for the widow" (1:17). Such commands and circumstances remind us that they, and we, live in a fallen, difficult world.

Second, the story reminds us that though God has given specific commands to help those who are weak, our leaders do not always obey this. Sin affects the hearts of individuals, and it also affects the government systems we have in place so that justice is not dispensed. The story of the unjust judge revealed a reality that was true in the ancient world and true in our modern world – judges and leaders often do not carry out their God-given responsibility to enact justice. Many are like the judge in the story who did not fear God and who did not respect man. This judge had no sense of honor and shame.

The prophet Isaiah, after he exhorted the people to dispense justice and to protect the weak said, "Your rulers are rebels and companions of thieves. Everyone loves a bribe and chases after rewards. They do not defend the orphan, nor does the widow's plea come before them" (Isaiah 1:23). Yes, our world is filled with fallen people and with fallen and sinful government systems that oppress the poor.

Third, the story tells us that even though we live in a fallen world, sometimes good things do happen. The widow in this story did get her wish! She did get legal protection and the reason she did was because of her *persistence* in crying out for it. Her persistence is a lesson for us to persist in our faith and in our prayer. This was the lesson Jesus gave to his disciples. Like the widow, don't give in to fear. Like the widow, keep crying out to God.

Many of us have fears that surround us. The disciples were fearful because Jesus kept talking about dying, and they knew if he was killed they would probably be killed too. But Jesus did not want them to give in to fear. Instead, he wanted them to pray.

What are your fears? Do you feel vulnerable and weak? Jesus encourages you to cry out to God day and night over those things that bother you, that trouble you, that make you afraid. Luke 18:1 tells us that Jesus told this story so that "at all times they should pray and not lose heart."

The New Testament is filled with exhortations to pray and to keep on praying. In Acts 1:14 we find that after Jesus was enthroned at the right hand of God, his followers met and devoted themselves to prayer. We find in Acts 2:42 that the first followers of Jesus devoted themselves to four things – teaching, worship, fellowship with one another, and praying. When the Church became very large, the apostles asked the members to appoint seven men to help them in caring for the widows in the church so that they could spend more time in prayer. Paul told the Roman Christians to devote themselves to prayer. To the Christians in Ephesus Paul said, "with all prayer and petition, pray at all times in the Spirit. Be on the alert with all prayer and petition for all of God's people." And to the Christians living in Colossae he said they should devote themselves to prayer, keeping alert in it with thanksgiving in their hearts."

For the disciples, a middle eastern widow crying out before a judge for legal protection was a familiar scene and would help them understand that they should cry out to God like that.

There is one more lesson for us. The unjust judge granted the woman her request, at last. Jesus wanted to drive home the point that our Father in heaven will grant our requests. He is not unjust. He is the righteous God. He is the just judge. He is the one from whom all just laws come. He does care for people. He is concerned about honor and shame. He does want to meet needs. He is not partial. He takes no bribes. He is full of love, concern, and compassion for the needs of all mankind. If the unjust judge could be moved by the constant pleas of a widow, how much more will the just judge of all the earth, the compassionate God, the heavenly Father be moved by the cries of his people!

God is not unjust. He is the righteous God. He is the just judge. He is the one from whom all just laws come. He does care for people. He is concerned about honor and shame. He does want to meet needs. He is not partial. He takes no bribes. He is full of love, concern, and compassion for the needs of all mankind.

Jesus guarantees that all prayers will be answered. Some will be answered quickly in our life. Some will not be answered until he returns, but justice will be done for all. Even though we come to him imperfectly, he has great patience with us. He is merciful and kind.

The widow who would not be silenced. A story of sorrow, a story of injustice, but a story of perseverance in crying out for what was right. It is a story to encourage us, to lift our hearts, and strengthen our faith. The question we must answer is, "When the Son of Man comes, will he find our hearts full of such faith?"

Read the Story as Originally Told in Luke 17:20-18:8

20 Now having been questioned by the Pharisees as to when the kingdom of God was coming, He answered them and said, "The kingdom of God is not coming with signs to be observed; 21 nor will they say, 'Look, here it is!' or, 'There it is!' For behold, the kingdom of God is in your midst."

22 And He said to the disciples, "The days will come when you will long to see one of the days of the Son of Man, and you will not see it. 23 They will say to you, 'Look there! Look here!' Do not go away, and do not run after them. 24 For just like the lightning, when it flashes out of one part of the sky, shines to the other part of the sky, so will the Son of Man be in His day. 25 But first He must suffer many things and be rejected by this generation. 26 And just as it happened in the days of Noah, so it will be also in the days of the Son of Man: 27 they were eating, they were drinking, they were marrying, they were being given in marriage, until the day that Noah entered the ark, and the flood came and destroyed them all. 28 It was the same as happened in the days of Lot: they were eating, they were drinking, they were buying, they were selling, they were planting, they were building; 29 but on the day that Lot went out from Sodom it rained fire and brimstone from heaven and destroyed them all. 30 It will be just the same on the day that the Son of Man is revealed. 31 On that day, the one who is on the housetop and whose goods are in the house must not go down to take them out; and likewise the one who is in the field must not turn back. *32* Remember Lot's wife. *33* Whoever seeks to keep his life will lose it, and whoever loses his life will preserve it. *34* I tell you, on that night there will be two in one bed; one will be taken and the other will be left. *35* There will be two women grinding at the same place; one will be taken and the other will be left. *36* Two men will be in the field; one will be taken and the other will be left." *37* And answering they said to Him, "Where, Lord?" And He said to them, "Where the body is, there also the vultures will be gathered."

1 Now He was telling them a parable to show that at all times they ought to pray and not to lose heart, *2* saying, "In a certain city there was a judge who did not fear God and did not respect man. *3* There was a widow in that city, and she kept coming to him, saying, 'Give me legal protection from my opponent.' *4* For a while he was unwilling; but afterward he said to himself, 'Even though I do not fear God nor respect man, *5* yet because this widow bothers me, I will give her legal protection, otherwise by continually coming she will wear me out.'" *6* And the Lord said, "Hear what the unrighteous judge said; *7* now, will not God bring about justice for His elect who cry to Him day and night, and will He delay long over them? *8* I tell you that He will bring about justice for them quickly. However, when the Son of Man comes, will He find faith on the earth?"

Cultural and Historical Insights

➢ In the Old Testament, King Jehoshaphat appointed judges to carry out the justice of God. But they could easily be corrupted or corrupt themselves. Amos spoke of such judges in 2:6-7 and 5:10-13 in his prophecy.

➤ Alfred Edersheim said, "judges in Jerusalem were called robber-judges rather than Prohibition Judges. In Aramaic or Hebrew this was a play upon words. The former being *Dayyaney Gezeloth* and the latter *Dayyaney Gezerot*."

➤ The Talmud speaks of village judges who were willing to pervert justice for a dish of meat.

➤ The judge's lack of respect for God and man has the sense of "he has no shame." He did not have the sense of shame or honor that ruled such cultures. Jeremiah speaks of prophets and priests who did not know how to blush. See Jeremiah 8:12.

➤ Verses on protecting widows are numerous in the Old Testament – Exodus 22:22-23; Deuteronomy 10:18, 24:17; 27:19; Job 22:9; 24:3, 21; Psalm 68:5; Isaiah 10:2; 1:17, 23.

➤ A widow would have no male protector in a male-dominated society. She would be extremely vulnerable. She would not normally have the strength to force her will. She would not have the money to buy justice.

➤ When the judge said the woman was wearing him out, this was a boxing term that meant to blacken the eye. The woman was bringing a blow to his head, not literally, but giving the man a headache. The judge is exaggerating but he is clearly irritated with her behavior.

➤ Continually coming – in the Greek it is *eis telos* – unto the *end*. The judge realizes that the women will never stop until he does something to help her.

These insights are from *Jesus Through Middle Eastern Eyes*, by Dr. Kenneth E. Bailey, IVP, 261-268.

Reflection

Jesus told the story of the widow to encourage the disciples. Evidently they were starting to become fearful and lose heart. Is there any fear that you have in your life? Are you in need of encouragement in any way?

_____

_____

_____

Describe some of the ways the widow would have been vulnerable. Do you believe you are vulnerable in any way?

_____

_____

_____

In what ways is God different from the unjust judge?

_____

_____

_____

Do you continually bring your requests before God?

_____

_____

_____

Jesus asked if he would find faith when he returns. Does he find faith in your heart right now?

_____

_____

_____

Listen to this story online at http://wgsministries.org/stories/ministry/. Click on **The Journey to Jerusalem** *(SM051-060)*, scroll down to **The Widow Who Would Not Be Silenced – SM054**, and play.

Caught in the Act of Sin!

Shame, anger, and hopelessness fill the heart of a woman caught in sin. Yes, she had done wrong, but so had the man and he was nowhere to be seen. Paraded through the Temple courts she is thrown at the feet of Jesus – guilty of adultery. Her fate will hang upon the words and actions of Jesus.

Jonathan Williams

8 CAUGHT IN THE ACT OF SIN

The religious leaders of the people were frustrated and angry. For months they had observed Jesus and they despised what they saw. He healed on the Sabbath. He did not ceremonially wash before meals. He invited sinful people to dine with him. He offered them forgiveness on the spot, as if he had authority to forgive.

Every time they brought up an objection to his work, he would reply with words of wisdom they could not answer. When they complained that he healed on the Sabbath, Jesus told them they performed circumcision on the Sabbath. Circumcision brought a child into the covenant with Abraham and made him officially part of the community of God's people. If they could bring a baby into the covenant community on the Sabbath, why was it wrong for him to restore people to full health by healing them on the Sabbath? If their own sons attempted to cast out evil spirits from people, why was it wrong for him to cast out evil spirits? They had no answer for his questions.

It was the Feast of Tabernacles and Jesus was teaching in the Temple. The people loved what he had to say about the kingdom of God. But the religious leaders hated it. They sent men to question him, but Jesus answered every question. They sent officers to arrest him, but when the officers arrived and heard him teach, they were left speechless and came back empty handed.

The leaders said, "Where is he? Where is Jesus? We sent you to arrest him and here you are before us with nothing?"

The officers said, "We have never heard anyone speak the way this man speaks, and now many of the people are saying he is the Messiah or the prophet that Moses said would come!"

"Don't tell me that you have been led astray. You don't see any of us believing in him do you? This crowd of uneducated people, they are under a curse. They don't know God's Word."

But one of the leaders of the people spoke up for Jesus. His name was Nicodemus. He had visited Jesus one night many months before and had asked Jesus face to face about his teaching and the things Jesus said had stirred his heart.

Nicodemus had come politely and said, "Jesus, many of us believe you have come from God. No one can do these miracles you are doing unless God is with him."

But Jesus got right to the heart of the matter with Nicodemus and said, "Nicodemus, you must be born again. I know you long for the kingdom of God to come but you cannot enter the kingdom of God unless you are born again."

Jesus, in so many words, told him that he had come for more than being a teacher in Israel. Jesus had come to change the hearts of people. Jesus had come to revolutionize lives from the inside out. People would not see the kingdom of God unless they were reborn, and when Nicodemus asked how that could be, Jesus explained that he was talking about a spiritual rebirth, about a work of the Spirit of God.

Nicodemus' life was never the same after that encounter with Jesus, and while his colleagues were deeply suspicious of Jesus and some had even concluded that Jesus must die, Nicodemus stood up for him and said:

"Our Law does not condemn a man unless it first hears from him and allows him to defend himself. You have already concluded he is guilty of breaking the Law of Moses but many of you have never even spoken to him and asked him to explain himself."

"Nicodemus! Search the Scriptures! Nowhere does it say a prophet arises out of Galilee. That is where he is from! He can't be from God if he is from Galilee. You are not from Galilee are you?"

Many of the leaders' laughed at the insult thrown at Nicodemus. But Nicodemus did not think it was funny, and he left the meeting. With nothing more to be said, the meeting adjourned, but unknown to Nicodemus and others was that some stayed and plotted to destroy Jesus. As they talked late into the night they came up with a plan to destroy him.

~~~

We don't know her name. We don't know how old she was. We don't know where she lived or what kind of upbringing she had or if she was in a marriage where she felt trapped. But the leaders in Jerusalem knew of her and they knew that she was an easy target for a man who wanted something on the side, for a man who was not content to be with his wife but who wanted to explore new areas of sexuality with other women.

That night she lay with a man who was not her husband. The woman never enjoyed it. It seemed exotic and exciting at first, to be with a man who was not her husband, and it brought some sense of belonging and being loved. But when the man was finished, she would often be left alone and a deep sense of shame, guilt, and emptiness would come over her. The same was true on this night. After she and the man had satisfied their desires, they slept together but sleep did not come easily for her. She felt lost, and she felt fear. She could not explain why she felt fear, but something was different about this encounter. The man who approached her insisted that he must have her that night and that he must stay with her.

Then she realized, "a trap." She started to get up but it was too late. She heard footsteps outside her house and then the door burst open and several men, dressed in long, religious robes walked into the room. "Is this your husband?" the men demanded.

"You know very well he is not my husband," she said.

"Then you know the Law, 'you shall not commit adultery.' You are under arrest for breaking the Law of God."

"Take her away and hold her until that rabbi from Galilee comes back into the Temple. We have quite a surprise for him."

"What about him?" the woman asked pointing to the man who was still on the bed. "It takes two to commit adultery." But the leaders just sneered at her and nodded to the officers who seized her arms and led her to the jail that would hold her until the strange trial would begin.

~~~

Jesus had spent the night outside Jerusalem. He had gone to the Mount of Olives just to the east of the city. It was a beautiful place and from this location he could look down upon the city from the booth he and others shared during the Feast of Tabernacles. But early in the morning he entered the city and the Temple. People saw him and he greeted and welcomed them. Then he began to teach them many things about the kingdom of God.

"The kingdom of God is not coming with a sword, but with seed. The kingdom of God is not coming to cut the bodies of men and bring them death. It comes to penetrate the hearts of people and bring them life the way a seed penetrates soil and brings a fruitful plant into the world.

"The kingdom of God is not coming with a great show of power to dazzle the leaders and to scare away the Romans, but it is coming in small steps and in small ways to change the lives of people and communities and nations from the inside out, just like a small mustard seed slowly grows into a large plant or just like yeast slowly but surely penetrates an entire lump of dough."

Everything seemed to be going so well. The people were enjoying his words and Jesus was enjoying teaching in his Father's temple. And then they heard a scream and some shouts.

"No, please, stop! This isn't fair! This isn't right!"

"Quiet woman and do as we say. You will get your trial!"

Many religious people were headed Jesus' way. Some were old and had been in their positions of power for decades. Others were young and full of energy and zeal for the ancestral traditions of their people. In their midst was a woman, her hair loose around her shoulders, the way it should not be in public. Her body barely covered with a light robe, as if she had been pulled out of bed, and her face filled with anger, fear and hopelessness.

The crowd parted to let them through. They went to Jesus and threw the woman down in front of him and said for all to hear,

"Teacher, this woman has been caught in adultery, in the very act. We are all witnesses. Now, in our Law, as you know, Moses commanded us to stone such women. And so we have brought her to you for your counsel. What do you say we should do with her?"

The hearts of the religious leaders were filled with glee. They had him. The woman before him had been caught sleeping with a man who was not her husband. This was not some vague "sinner" who could claim that she had repented. This was not some poor person who was lamenting mistakes in life to whom he could pronounce forgiveness. This was a woman who had a reputation, this was a woman who was a fresh sinner, who had just been caught in the very act.

Here was the trap. If Jesus offered forgiveness, as he had offered to so many, they could accuse him of not obeying the Law of Moses, and the people would not support him. They knew the laws of God. They knew adultery was wrong and was punishable by death. And if Jesus did not uphold this law, the leaders knew the people would stop following him. They could arrest him on the spot for counseling rebellion against this clear teaching.

But if Jesus did not forgive, then he would be seen as compromising his teaching. He had come offering salvation and forgiveness to all. He had come offering a fresh start to all. Could he offer a fresh start to this woman? She was caught in the very act! She was caught defying the laws of the God of Israel.

Clearly Jesus was in a tough situation. The religious leaders stood defiantly before him. They had made their case powerful and simple. The woman had been caught just hours before in a bed of adultery.

The crowd who had been sitting and listening to Jesus now stood and drew near to see what Jesus would do.

The woman lay prostrate before Jesus weeping for the injustice done to her. She felt used – not just by the man with whom she had slept but by the powerful who were using her as a tool to get at Jesus. They would sacrifice her life in order to accuse and kill this teacher. Yes, she was an adulteress, but they were manipulators, plotters, schemers, murderers. But they were not on trial. Nor was the man with whom she had sinned anywhere around. She was just a woman. What could she say and what could she do? She was helpless. She was powerless.

Jesus looked upon the leaders. He looked upon the crowd. He looked upon the woman and then he stooped down and began to write something on the ground as if he were not paying attention to what had just been said and done right in front of him.

The leaders watched for a moment and then in exasperation said again, "Jesus. We asked you a question, and as the spiritual leaders of these people, we have a right to hear an answer from you. This woman was caught in the very act of adultery. Moses commanded us to stone such women. We have brought her before you. Tell us what we should do."

Jesus stopped writing on the ground. He stood up again and

looking directly into the faces of the men he said, "Let the one among you who is without sin be the first to cast a stone at her." Then he stooped back down and began writing on the ground again.

All became quiet. The leaders looked at one another and realized that their trap for Jesus had been sprung on them. They had caught the woman in the very act of adultery. But Jesus had caught them in the very act of deception and lies in order to kill. The Law that said "you shall not commit adultery" also said "You shall not murder" and "you shall not bear false witness against your neighbor." They knew they were as guilty as she was and they knew that Jesus saw into their hearts.

Their plan had been exposed. Besides, it was easy for everyone to see through it anyway. If they caught the woman in the very act of adultery then they should have caught the man, but where was the guilty man who had slept with this woman? But more than their misstep and oversight and glaring hole in their argument was the deep searing conviction they felt for their plotting and their scheming and their leading this woman into sin in order to get at Jesus.

One by one the religious leaders walked away, starting with the wiser, older ones and ending with the young zealots who were men of action and not very smart. One by one these men walked away, heads down and defeated, faces full of shame, and hearts full of turmoil.

Oh, if only they had fallen on their faces before Jesus! Oh, if only they had fallen to the ground with the woman and asked for her forgiveness and asked Jesus for mercy! How the story might have changed. But they were too proud for that. One by one, from the oldest to the youngest, the men just walked away.

All eyes watched as they exited the Temple, and then all eyes turned back to Jesus and to the woman who was still before him. What would Jesus do now? What would he say? She was still guilty. She was not denying her sin.

Jesus stopped writing on the ground. He stood back up, looked upon the woman and said, "Woman, where are your accusers? Has no one condemned you?"

The woman stood up. She wiped the tears from her face. She looked around and saw that all the men were gone. Those moments when she was at the feet of Jesus and when she heard their words of condemnation had seemed like an eternity to her. Now as she looked around she saw that all of her accusers were gone. She said to Jesus with astonishment in her voice, "There is no one, Lord. They are all gone. The ones who have condemned me are gone."

And then the one who was sinless, the one who could have condemned her, the one who could have cast the first and the last stone said, "Neither do I condemn you. Go. From now on, sin no more."

And the woman wrapped her light garment around herself and with indescribable relief and astonishment and joy walked through the crowd and went home – a new person who had been touched by the grace of Jesus.

~~~

The woman who was caught in adultery – I hope you know that this story is really a story about all of us. All of us are like the woman or like the religious leaders. Which are you like? Are you like the the religious leaders who are critical, judging and trying to bring others down rather than restoring and helping those in need? If you are, if that is your tendency, prepare for Jesus to expose your hypocrisy and prepare to slink away as quietly as you can, unless, you fall before him and confess your sins and failures and ask for his mercy.

All of us are like the woman who stands before Jesus guilty of our sins. In the final scene of our story the woman was left alone before Jesus. She who was full of sin was before him who was sinless. Ultimately you and I will stand alone before Jesus with our sins exposed.

Most of us are probably like the woman. If we have not committed adultery with our bodies, the likelihood is great that we have committed adultery in our hearts. Jesus said, "You have heard that it was said, 'You shall not commit adultery.' But I say to you that everyone who looks at a woman with lust for her has already committed adultery with her in his heart."

If it is not adultery, then it is something else. All of us have sinned.

What is your sin? What is your weakness? Do you know what Jesus said on another occasion about this? He said, "It is not the things that come into the person that defile a person, but the things that come from the heart. Those defile the man. For out of the heart come evil thoughts, murders, adulteries, fornications, thefts, false witness, slanders. These are the things which defile the man."

Jesus could have picked any number of sins. There are so many. And we have committed them.

Yes, none of us can cast the first stone and all of us are like the woman who stands before Jesus guilty of our sins. In the final scene of our story the woman was left alone before Jesus. She who was full of sin was before him who was sinless. And whether we identify with the woman in the story or with the religious leaders who walked away in shame doesn't really matter because ultimately you and I will stand alone before Jesus with our sins exposed.

> There is really only one opinion that counts and one opinion we need to worry about. It's not our accusers. It's not our fellow humans. It is the opinion and the verdict of Jesus.

You and I must realize there is really only one opinion that counts and one opinion we need to worry about. It's not our accusers. It's not our fellow humans. It is the opinion and the verdict of Jesus who is the Judge of all for God has fixed a day in which he will judge the world in righteousness through Jesus whom he has appointed as Judge, having furnished proof to all men by raising him from the dead.

Jesus is Lord. Jesus is the Judge and he is the Lord because he has risen from the dead, but I have indescribably good news for you. When he died, he died for our sins that we might be forgiven. And when he rose it was proof that nothing more had to be done to pay for our sins. It is as if he were stoned for the woman. When he took the nails in his hands and feet it was for her sins and your sins and mine. And when he rose from the grave, it was proof that everything that needed to be done to save us from condemnation had been done.

To this woman he said, "I do not condemn you. Go and do not engage in this activity again. Go and do not sin, but you may go and you may now live in freedom."

To us he says, "I do not condemn you." And when he says "go and sin no more" to us, he means that we are to go into a new life and into a new way where we learn to follow God and learn to live in obedience to him.

Many people left the presence of Jesus on that day. The woman left the presence of Jesus a new person. The religious leaders left the presence of Jesus, but they were the same hardened, proud, self righteous men. The woman humbled herself. The men remained convinced of their cause against Jesus. The woman heard the freeing words of Jesus. The men could have heard such words if they had remained and begged Jesus for mercy, but they chose to walk away from the presence of Christ.

That is a picture of the world. Some remain before Jesus and wait for his word of mercy. Some walk away and harden their hearts. Some will walk away for eternity and never hear his offer of peace and forgiveness because of the stubbornness of their soul.

Have you heard Jesus say to you, "Neither do I condemn you. Go and sin no more"? Have you experienced Jesus' mercy and forgiveness for all you have done wrong? I pray that you have. I pray you will not be like those men who used this woman to get at Jesus and who were too proud to humble themselves before him and walked away without hearing his words of mercy.

Why not call upon Jesus today? Why not say, "Jesus, I am like this woman. I have sinned. I need your mercy. Thank you for dying on the cross for me. Thank you for taking the condemnation in my place. I receive your forgiveness. I will follow you in this new life."

Which example will you follow today?

Read the Story as Originally Told in John 7:40-8:11

Some of the people therefore, when they heard these words, were saying, "This certainly is the Prophet." [41] Others were saying, "This is the Christ." Still others were saying, "Surely the Christ is not going to come from Galilee, is He? [42] Has not the Scripture said that the Christ comes from the descendants of David, and from Bethlehem, the village where David was?" [43] So a division occurred in the crowd because of Him. [44] Some of them wanted to seize Him, but no one laid hands on Him.

[45] The officers then came to the chief priests and Pharisees, and they said to them, "Why did you not bring Him?" [46] The officers answered, "Never has a man spoken the way this man speaks." [47] The Pharisees then answered them, "You have not also been led astray, have you? [48] No one of the rulers or Pharisees has believed in Him, has he? [49] But this crowd which does not know the Law is accursed." [50] Nicodemus (he who came to Him before, being one of them) said to them, [51] "Our Law does not judge a man unless it first hears from him and knows what he is doing, does it?" [52] They answered him, "You are not also from Galilee, are you? Search, and see that no prophet arises out of Galilee [53] Everyone went to his home.

[1] But Jesus went to the Mount of Olives. [2] Early in the morning He came again into the temple, and all the people were coming to Him; and He sat down and began to teach them. [3] The scribes and the Pharisees brought a woman caught in adultery, and having set her in the center of the court, [4] they said to Him, "Teacher, this woman has been caught in adultery, in the very act. [5] Now in the

Law, Moses commanded us to stone such women; what then do You say?" [6] They were saying this, testing Him, so that they might have grounds for accusing Him. But Jesus stooped down and with His finger wrote on the ground. [7] But when they persisted in asking Him, He straightened up, and said to them, "He who is without sin among you, let him be the first to throw a stone at her." [8] Again He stooped down and wrote on the ground. [9] When they heard it, they began to go out one by one, beginning with the older ones, and He was left alone, and the woman, where she was, in the center of the court. [10] Straightening up, Jesus said to her, "Woman, where are they? Did no one condemn you?" [11] She said, "No one, Lord." And Jesus said, "I do not condemn you, either. Go. From now on sin no more."

Cultural and Historical Insights

➤ The Mount of Olives is a mile-long ridge of limestone hills to the east of Jerusalem and was still within the jurisdiction of the city of Jerusalem.

➤ In ancient times, the coming of each new moon was announced by signals from the mount.

➤ Jesus most likely erected a small booth on the mount for the celebration of the Feast of Tabernacles.

➤ The Mount of Olives is the biblical site of apocalyptic prophecy in Zechariah 14:4-5 and the place from which Jesus gave his great discourse about the end (See Matthew 24-25).

➤ Acts 21:28 mentions a Jewish false prophet who sought to launch an attack on Jerusalem from the Mount of Olives.

> The committing of adultery was forbidden in the Ten Commandments (Exodus 20:14) and was punishable by death (Leviticus 20:10).

These insights were gleaned from *The Words and Works of Jesus Christ*, J. Dwight Pentecost, Zondervan, 282-83, *Wycliffe's Historical Geography of Bible Lands* by Pfeiffer and Vos, Moody Press, 158-59, and *Dictionary of Jesus and the Gospels*, IVP, 43-44.

Reflection

In the beginning of this story, Nicodemus defended Jesus against the religious leaders. Read Nicodemus' first encounter with Jesus in John 3:1-16 and explain how that conversation with Jesus would have affected him in a positive way to defend him.

_____

_____

_____

The religious leaders said the woman was caught in the very act. Do you think this implies that they plotted to catch her in this act in order to bring her to Jesus? Why do you think they did not bring the man?

_____

_____

_____

Twice the story says Jesus was writing on the ground. Why do you think he did this? What do you think he was writing?

_____

_____

_____

The story tells us that the men left, from the oldest to the youngest. Why do you think it was in this order?

_____

_____

_____

Jesus did not condemn the woman but he also told her to go and sin no more. What is the relationship between forgiveness and living a holy life? Should one lead to the other?

_____

_____

_____

Listen to this story online at http://wgsministries.org/stories/ministry/. Click on **Conflict in Israel** *(SM031-040)*, scroll down to **Caught in the Act of Sin – SM034**, and play.

The Grieving Sisters of Bethany

Martha, Mary, and Lazarus loved Jesus and how he loved them! When Lazarus becomes deathly ill the sisters send word for him to come and heal their brother. But Jesus arrives late and Lazarus is four days in his tomb. When Jesus speaks to the grieving sisters, he tells them something they and the whole world must hear.

Jonathan Williams

9 THE GRIEVING SISTERS
OF BETHANY

Just over the Mount of Olives, not quite two miles from Jerusalem lay a small village named Bethany. We have heard about Bethany already. We have learned that it was an important town in Israel. According to the Temple Scroll, one of the documents known as the Dead Sea Scrolls, the Jews designated three places east of Jerusalem to care for the sick. One of these was Bethany. In their purity rules, the Jews established a perimeter around Jerusalem saying nothing unclean should come within that boundary. Jerusalem, above all, must remain a holy city. But the sick did need care and Bethany was an ideal location for it was close to the great city but outside the perimeter established by the religious leaders. Because it was to the southeast of the Mount of Olives, it could not be seen from Jerusalem, and because it was out of sight, it was a suitable place to care for the sick.

We have also learned that Bethany was also a favorite site for pilgrims travelling from the north in Galilee. In order not to come into contact with the hated Samaritans, the Jews would bypass

Samaria to the east of the Jordan River, come to Jericho, and then traverse up the steep road and lodge in Bethany, the final stop before coming to Jerusalem.

In this lovely town which was famous for its hospitality as well as for its care for the sick, was a family that Jesus loved. In this family was a man by the name of Lazarus who lived with his two sisters, Martha and Mary. Jesus had enjoyed their hospitality before and had come to love the industrious Martha, the contemplative Mary, and their brother Lazarus. Mary and Martha would never forget the words that Jesus said to them on that occasion. "Friends, rarely have I received such warm and loving hospitality in Israel. You have ministered greatly to me. I want you to know that I will always have you in my heart. I will always love you." Jesus then placed his hand on Lazarus' shoulder, looked deep into his soul, and said, "Lazarus, no matter what happens, you must know that I will never stop loving you and your sisters. You will always have a special place in my heart."

One night, many months after that memorable visit, Lazarus told his sisters, "Martha, Mary, I am going to retire early. I don't know what's wrong with me. My head hurts and I don't feel well."

"Sleep well, brother. The Lord's peace be with you. When you awaken may you find his mercies and be in good health."

But the next morning, Lazarus did not awaken. His sisters were up and about their business in the house and when they did not see Lazarus they became concerned. They went to the doorway of his room and said softly, "Lazarus, Lazarus, are you alright?" But all they heard was a groan. The sisters immediately ran to his bedside and found Lazarus burning with a fever. They had never felt such fever-heat before.

Because Bethany was famous for its care for the sick, many people were well-practiced in caring for different illnesses. The sisters asked for some of these specialists to come and examine their brother, confident they would know what to do. But they were not prepared for the news they would hear. "Your brother is gravely ill. Whenever we have tended anyone with such a fever and with his other symptoms, well … it would take a miracle. I fear that his time is near. His life is in the hands of God alone."

The sisters burst into tears. "No, this cannot be. He was fine yesterday. Only last night he complained of his head hurting and not feeling well. How can this be?" But the specialist could only say, "I'm sorry. We will pray."

As Mary wept, Martha called all of the servants together and said, "Everyone listen. Lazarus, our brother is gravely ill. He may not last through the day. Do any of you know where Jesus is? Have any of you heard of his whereabouts?"

One of the servants said, "Yes, I believe he is not too far away in a village. He has been travelling east of the Jordan and has been making his way in this direction. This is what I have heard."

"Then go as quickly as you can and bring him here. Tell, him that Lazarus, the one he dearly loves is sick and near to death." Then the sisters went to their brother's room and tended to his care, praying that the servants would find Jesus and that he would come in time, and watching as their brother grew weaker and his breathing shallower.

The servants prepared for their journey and headed in the direction where they thought they would find Jesus. They went through many villages and inquired as to his whereabouts. Finally someone said, "Yes, Jesus has been staying in that house over there. In fact, last night he hosted a great dinner for many people. You will find him there."

The servants were filled with joy when they heard the news and as they approached they recognized some of the men who were Jesus' disciples. "Please, sirs, we must see Jesus."

"Who are you and what do you want?" Peter asked.

"We are servants of Lazarus and his sisters Martha and Mary. You stayed with us, and your master, Jesus, taught in their house some months ago."

"Yes, yes, I recognize you now and I remember them. Is all well?"

"Sir, the sisters have sent us with urgent news. Their brother Lazarus is sick. They fear for his life. They have sent us with this message," and they handed a small scroll to Peter. On it were written the words, "Lord, behold, the one whom you love is sick."

Just then Jesus emerged from the house and the servants said, "Master, rabbi, please hear us, Lazarus, the one that you dearly love is sick. We fear that he dying."

Jesus looked at his disciples and then he turned to the servants and said, "Go, tell them that this sickness is not to end in death. Tell them that his sickness is so that God may be glorified. Tell them that I, the anointed one, the Son of God will find glory through this sickness."

The servants were overjoyed at this news and they said, "Thank you master, thank you rabbi." And as they prepared to return home they paused and looked at Jesus and said, "Well, master, are you coming with us to Lazarus' home?"

Jesus said, "Tell them this sickness will not end in death. Tell them my Father and I will be glorified by it. Now go." Then Jesus went back into the house and prayed.

In Bethany, the sisters continued to care for their brother. From time to time Martha would go to the entrance of their house and look anxiously down the road for a sign of their servants. Then she would return to her brother's bedside, and Mary would say, "Is there any sign of them sister? Will they find Jesus? Will Jesus come?"

Finally, many hours later, as they began to lose hope they heard the sound they had been waiting for. The servants had returned! Martha hurried to the courtyard as the servants were dismounting.

"We have such good news for you Martha! We found him! He said that your brother's sickness would not end in death. He said that his sickness was for the glory of God."

"But, but, where is Jesus?" Martha asked. "Why did you not bring Jesus with you? Lazarus is not better. Lazarus is dying. God has not healed him."

Just then they heard a loud wail come from the house. It was the voice of Mary, crying out with anguish. Lazarus was dead.

~~~

After the servants left Jesus and his disciples, with joy, thinking that Lazarus would be healed, the disciples said, "Well, Master, are we going to Bethany or not?" But Jesus kept quiet and said nothing and the disciples waited and wondered why Jesus gave such assurances to the servants but did not immediately travel with them to heal his beloved friend. One of them said, "do you remember a couple of years ago, when we were in Cana? Do you remember that official who came and told us about his sick son in Capernaum? Jesus didn't go with him and yet his son was healed without Jesus even going there. Maybe Jesus did the same with Lazarus."

Another said, "Yes, but perhaps Jesus does not want to go to Bethany. Bethany is in Judea and only a couple of miles from Jerusalem. The religious leaders are angry with him over the stories he has been telling and all he has been doing. And you remember what happened the last time we were there, they wanted to stone him."

After two days Jesus surprised them all and said, "Prepare your belongings. It's time. We are going to Judea again and first we must stop in Bethany."

"But teacher," one of the disciples said, "you do know what happened the last time we were in Judea. The leaders tried to kill you. They wanted to stone you. Are you sure you want to go there again?"

Jesus replied, "how many hours of daylight are there in a day? Twelve? Yes. That is the time to do the work of God, when it is daylight. If you try to walk when it is night you will stumble in the darkness. But if we go while it is light, we won't stumble. Besides, our friend, Lazarus, awaits us. He has fallen into a deep sleep, and I go to awaken him from sleep."

The disciples breathed a sigh of relief. "Lord, this is such good news about Lazarus, that he has fallen asleep. If he is asleep he will recover. He will be healed."

But Jesus said, "You don't understand. When I said that Lazarus has fallen asleep, I did not mean that he was just asleep. Lazarus is dead. Lazarus died shortly after the servants were here."

"What?" the disciples said, "But you said Lazarus' sickness was not to end in death. You said his sickness would be to the glory of God. You sent the servants away thinking Lazarus would be restored to health and now you say he died?"

Jesus replied, "I am so glad, for your sakes, I was not there. I am building your faith. I want you to believe like you have never before believed. You must trust me. Let's go. We're going to Judea and there we will find death."

The disciples shuddered at the mention of death and at the memory of the hatred of those who wanted to kill Jesus. Now, Jesus was saying they must go back to this place and that death was waiting. What did he mean? It sounded so ominous. Lazarus was not healed. Lazarus died. Jesus knew the religious leaders were looking for him and that they wanted to kill him. It seemed that Jesus was walking into a trap.

~~~

In Bethany, the sisters and the servants were grieving. Many friends and family members had come to be with them at this time. It had been several days since Lazarus became ill and since the sisters sent the desperate plea for Jesus to come and heal their brother. But Jesus had not healed him. Jesus had not even come. Lazarus, their beloved brother was dead.

The servants had washed his body. They wrapped it in linen cloths, placing spices within the folds of the garments. They carried his body outside the village to a cave owned by the family.

This is where other family members had been placed. Now Lazarus was placed with them on a ledge hewn into the rock. A stone was rolled against the opening, and the sisters returned home weeping over the sudden loss of their brother.

Often the sisters were given to fits of weeping and wailing over their loss and the attempts to comfort them seemed futile. Their grief mounted higher as they thought of what Jesus could have done, if he had only come with the servants. Then, someone said, "Martha, Mary. He is coming. Jesus is coming. He is headed for the place of burial and he wants you to come to him."

"What? He is coming now? Why now?"

"Jesus is calling for you."

And when the sisters heard this news Martha immediately got up to see him but Mary stayed back. "You go Martha. I cannot go to that tomb. Not yet. I cannot go see Jesus. My heart is too heavy."

And so Martha went alone to see Jesus. She had so many questions and so many emotions going through her heart. She felt anger. Jesus had healed so many other people. Why could he not have healed her brother? She felt unloved. Why did Jesus stay away? Why did Jesus not come? She felt confusion. Why did he come now?

When she saw him she ran to him and with sorrow in her voice said, "Lord, Lord, why did you not come? If you had been here my brother would not have died. I have believed in you. I believe that even now, whatever you ask of God he will give you. I believe if Lazarus were still alive you could ask God and he would hear your prayer and heal him. But you didn't come."

"Martha, your brother will rise again."

"Oh Lord, I know he will rise again. I know that on the last day, the great day at the end of the age, God will raise him and everyone else. He will rise again with all God's people."

"Martha, I am the resurrection and the life. He who believes in me will live again, even if he dies. Everyone who lives and believes in me will never die. Do you believe this, that I am the resurrection, that I am the life?"

Martha, wiped away her tears. She stood up. She looked at Jesus' face. There was such compassion in his eyes, such tenderness in his voice, such conviction in his words, and she said, "Yes, Lord, I believe that you are Messiah, you are the Son of God, the King, you are the one we have all been waiting for."

Jesus asked, "Where is Mary?" And Martha said, "She didn't want to come. She said she wasn't ready to come to this tomb, and she said she wasn't ready to see you."

Jesus looked with great sadness upon Martha and said, "Martha, go get Mary and bring her here," and Martha went home and said quietly to Mary, "Mary, Jesus is calling for you again. He insists that you meet him at the tomb. I will go back with you." And so Mary got up to go with her sister, and when the friends and family members who had come to console her saw her get up, they decided to go to the tomb with her. They thought she was going to weep over Lazarus, and they would weep with her.

When Mary arrived, they saw her fall at the feet of Jesus and say with a very loud voice, "Lord, if you had been here my brother would not have died. I have believed in you. I believe that even now, whatever you ask of God he will give you. I believe if Lazarus were still alive you could ask God and he would hear your prayer and heal him. But you did not come."

Then the entire company of people began to mourn over Lazarus. It seemed the whole world was weeping over the death of this man. Jesus looked upon them all. He saw their grief. He saw their sorrow. He saw their pain. And then Jesus said,

"Where have you laid him?" And they said, "Lord, come and see." They took Jesus to the cave where Lazarus had been laid four days earlier, and when he saw the place he was overcome with grief for his friend, and Jesus burst into tears and wept with all those who were weeping.

When the friends of Martha and Mary saw Jesus weeping at the burial site they said, "Look, look at how he weeps. Behold how he loved Lazarus. Jesus is overcome with grief for our friend and brother."

Another said, "We have heard so many stories of this man. He has healed so many people. He has even given sight to the blind. Could not this man, if he had been here, could he not have healed Lazarus? Could not Jesus have kept him from dying? If only he had come in time!"

Jesus listened for a few moments. He listened to what the people were saying. He listened to their words of pain. He listened to their hearts that had been disappointed. He listened to their weeping and sorrow. And then, being deeply moved within his heart he walked to the cave entrance. The stone was exactly where it had been placed four days earlier, against the entrance to the burial cave, and Jesus said,

"Remove the stone."

Martha looked at Jesus and said, "Lord, by this time there will be a stench. He has been dead four days."

But Jesus turned to Martha and to his disciples and said, "Did I not say that if you believe, you will see the glory of God? Remove the stone!"

So they removed the stone and stood back, waiting to see what Jesus would do next. He lifted his hands to heaven and said in a loud voice, "Father, I thank you that you have heard my prayer. I know that you always hear me but for the sake of all those with me I say this – thank you for hearing my prayer – so that they may believe that you have sent me."

Jesus finished. He looked toward the tomb and his face was full of anger at death. His face full of fury at sorrow. His face full of anguish over the pain of all mankind. He sighed deeply, and then in a loud voice he said,

"Lazarus, come forth!"

Martha and Mary looked at each other with astonishment. They looked at Jesus. They looked at the entrance of the cave. The crowd was silent. All held their breath, and then they saw him, Lazarus standing at the cave entrance, burial cloths wrapped around him, walking, breathing, and alive!

Jesus said, "Go to him and loose his garments. Your brother lives!" And the people shouted and wept, but this time they wept for joy!

~~~

Oh my friends, if we could have been there, if we could have seen the grief and the anguish of the sisters, their friends and their family. If we could have been there and seen Jesus weeping. If we could have been there and seen Jesus praying. If we could have been there and seen his anger over death which robs us all. If we could have been there and heard his voice, "Lazarus, come forth." If we could have been there and seen Lazarus raised from the dead! What would that have been like? But we were not there. We are here. What do we learn from it?

What do you believe about Jesus? Do you believe he was a great teacher? That is good. But you must believe more. Do you believe he was a great healer? That is good. But you must believe more. Do you believe he was a great prophet? That is good. But you must believe more. You must believe that Jesus is the Lord of life!

Have you ever been by the side of someone who has died? I'm sure many of you have. I, too. I was at the side of my father when he died. I was at the side of my mother, holding her hand when she died. They were both old, advanced in years, and had lived a full life to the glory of God. It was not easy, but we knew it was their time.

Have you ever been by the side of someone that you loved dearly and you said, "Why Lord? Why now? This cannot be her time?" This happened to me many years ago when my first wife, in the prime of her life succumbed to the ravages of cancer. How can God allow such a thing to happen? We all must die, but why must some die young? Why must some die before they have had a chance to live the full number of days we thought were allotted to us all?

Such was the case with Lazarus. His sickness and his death were a shock to the entire family. He must not have been an old man nor his sisters old women. They were all in the fullness of life and doing well. Lazarus' sickness was completely unexpected, and it seemed that, according to Jesus's words, he would get better. Jesus had said that his sickness was not to end in death, yet Lazarus died. Why?

Jesus purposely was late. Jesus allowed Lazarus to die so that he could teach them, and us, a greater lesson. They all believed Jesus was a healer. But their faith needed to grow. They needed to believe in Jesus as the one who raises the dead and as the one who gives life, as the one who is the resurrection and the life.

What do you believe about Jesus? Do you believe he was a great teacher? That is good. But you must believe more. Do you believe he was a great healer? That is good. But you must believe more. Do you believe he was a great prophet? That is good. But you must believe more. You must believe that Jesus is the Lord of life! You must believe that Jesus is the one who has power over all sickness, all sorrow, all evil spirits, all sin, and that he has power even over death. Jesus is Lord and no one else.

Read the Story as Originally Told in John 11:1-46

Now a certain man was sick, Lazarus of Bethany, the village of Mary and her sister Martha. [2] It was the Mary who anointed the Lord with ointment, and wiped His feet with her hair, whose brother Lazarus was sick. [3] So the sisters sent word to Him, saying, "Lord, behold, he whom You love is sick." [4] But when Jesus heard this, He said, "This sickness is not to end in death, but for the glory of God, so that the Son of God may be glorified by it." [5] Now Jesus loved Martha and her sister and Lazarus. [6] So when He heard that he was sick, He then stayed two days longer in the place where He was. [7] Then after this He said to the disciples, "Let us go to Judea again." [8] The disciples said to Him, "Rabbi, the Jews were just now seeking to stone You, and are You going there again?" [9] Jesus answered, "Are there not twelve hours in the day? If anyone walks in the day, he does not stumble, because he sees the light of this world. [10] But if anyone walks in the night, he stumbles, because the light is not in him." [11] This He said, and after that He said to them, "Our friend Lazarus has fallen asleep; but I go, so that I may awaken him out of sleep." [12] The disciples then said to Him, "Lord, if he has fallen asleep, he will recover." [13] Now Jesus had spoken of his death, but they thought that He was speaking of literal sleep. [14] So Jesus then said to them plainly, "Lazarus is dead, [15] and I am glad for your sakes that I was not there, so that you may believe; but let us go to him." [16] Therefore Thomas, who is called Didymus, said to his fellow disciples, "Let us also go, so that we may die with Him."

[17] So when Jesus came, He found that he had already been in the tomb four days. [18] Now Bethany was near Jerusalem, about two miles off; [19] and many of the Jews had come to Martha and Mary, to console them concerning their brother. [20] Martha therefore, when she heard that Jesus was coming, went to meet Him, but Mary stayed at the house. [21] Martha then said to Jesus, "Lord, if You had been here, my brother would not have died. [22] Even now I know that whatever You ask of God, God will give You." [23] Jesus said to her, "Your brother will rise again." [24] Martha said to Him, "I know that he will rise again in the resurrection on the last day." [25] Jesus said to her, "I am the resurrection and the life; he who believes in Me will live even if he dies, [26] and everyone who lives and believes in Me will never die. Do you believe this?" [27] She said to Him, "Yes, Lord; I have believed that You are the Christ, the Son of God, even He who comes into the world." [28] When she had said this, she went away and called Mary her sister, saying secretly,

"The Teacher is here and is calling for you." [29] *And when she heard it, she got up quickly and was coming to Him.*

[30] *Now Jesus had not yet come into the village, but was still in the place where Martha met Him.* [31] *Then the Jews who were with her in the house, and consoling her, when they saw that Mary got up quickly and went out, they followed her, supposing that she was going to the tomb to weep there.* [32] *Therefore, when Mary came where Jesus was, she saw Him, and fell at His feet, saying to Him, "Lord, if You had been here, my brother would not have died."* [33] *When Jesus therefore saw her weeping, and the Jews who came with her also weeping, He was deeply moved in spirit and was troubled,* [34] *and said, "Where have you laid him?" They said to Him, "Lord, come and see."* [35] *Jesus wept.* [36] *So the Jews were saying, "See how He loved him!"* [37] *But some of them said, "Could not this man, who opened the eyes of the blind man, have kept this man also from dying?"*

[38] *So Jesus, again being deeply moved within, came to the tomb. Now it was a cave, and a stone was lying against it.* [39] *Jesus said, "Remove the stone." Martha, the sister of the deceased, said to Him, "Lord, by this time there will be a stench, for he has been dead four days."* [40] *Jesus said to her, "Did I not say to you that if you believe, you will see the glory of God?"* [41] *So they removed the stone. Then Jesus raised His eyes, and said, "Father, I thank You that You have heard Me.* [42] *I knew that You always hear Me; but because of the people standing around I said it, so that they may believe that You sent Me."* [43] *When He had said these things, He cried out with a loud voice, "Lazarus, come forth."* [44] *The man who had died came forth, bound hand and foot with wrappings, and his face was wrapped around with a cloth. Jesus said to them, "Unbind him, and let him go."*

45 Therefore many of the Jews who came to Mary, and saw what He had done, believed in Him. 46 But some of them went to the Pharisees and told them the things which Jesus had done.

Cultural and Historical Insights

Ancient Bethany was the site of an almshouse for the poor and a place of care for the sick. There is a hint of association between Bethany and care for the unwell in the Gospels: Mark tells of Simon the Leper's house there (Mark 14:3-10); Jesus receives urgent word of Lazarus' illness from Bethany (John 11:1-12:11).

According to the Temple Scroll from Qumran, three places for the care of the sick, including one for lepers, are to be located to the east of Jerusalem. The passage also defines a (minimum) radius of three thousand cubits (circa 1,800 yards) around the city within which nothing unclean shall be seen (XLVI:13-18). Since Bethany was, according to John, fifteen stadia (about 1.72 miles) from the holy city, care for the sick there corresponded with the requirements of the Temple Scroll (the stadion being ideally 600 feet (180 m) or 400 cubits). Whereas Bethphage is probably to be identified with At-Tur, located on the peak of the Mount of Olives with a magnificent view of Jerusalem, Bethany lay below to the southeast, out of view of the Temple Mount, which may have made its location suitable as a place for care of the sick, "out of view" of the Temple.

From this it is possible to deduce that the mention of Simon the Leper at Bethany in Mark's Gospel suggests that the Essenes, or pious patrons from Jerusalem who held to a closely similar view of ideal arrangements, settled lepers at Bethany. Such influence on the planning of Jerusalem and its environs (and even its Temple) may have been possible especially during the reign of Herod the Great (36-4 B.C.), whose favour towards the Essenes was noted by Josephus (*Antiquities* 15.10.5 [373-8]).

Reta Halteman Finger approves Capper's judgment that only in the context of an almshouse at Bethany, where the poor were received and assisted, could Jesus remark that "The poor you will always have with you" (Mark 14:7; Matthew 26:11) without sounding callous. Ling follows Capper's thesis concerning the connection between then place-name Bethany and the location there of an almshouse. Capper and Ling note that it is only in Bethany we find mention of the poor on the lips of the disciples, who object that the expensive perfumed oil poured over Jesus there might have been sold and the proceeds given to the poor (Mark 14:5; Matthew 26:8-9; John 12:4-6 [where the objection is made by Judas]); this objection may have been made in embarrassment and may also suggest a special connection between Bethany and care for the poor

It has also been suggested, based on the names found carved on thousands of ossuaries at the site, that Bethany in the time of Jesus was settled by people from Galilee who had come to live by Jerusalem. This would explain why Jesus and the disciples, as Galileans, would find it convenient to stay here when visiting Jerusalem.

These insights were taken from the article on *Bethany* by Brian J. Capper, "Essene Community Houses and Jesus' Early Community" (2006), in James H. Charlesworth, ed., *Jesus and Archaeology, 474-502*, Eerdmans, and quoted in Wikipedia.

Reflection

Luke 10:38-42 tells us about Jesus' previous visit to the home of Lazarus, Martha, and Mary. At that time there was conflict between Martha and Mary. Yet, we find they are still greatly loved by Jesus in this story. What does this tell us about the love of Jesus for people, even though they have problems?

_____

_____

_____

When Mary and Martha sent word that their brother Lazarus was sick, do you believe they were confident Jesus would come? How do you think they felt when Jesus did not arrive in time, and seemed purposely to stay away?

_____

_____

_____

Have you ever felt like God has not answered your prayers, or is late? How does that make you feel? Does this story encourage your heart in any way?

_____

_____

_____

Why do you think Jesus said "this sickness is not for death but for the glory of God?" In what way did it show God's glory?

_____

_____

_____

What did the people believe about Jesus before Lazarus died? What did the people believe about Jesus after he raised Lazarus? What do you believe about Jesus?

_____

_____

_____

Listen to this story online at http://wgsministries.org/stories/ministry/. Click on The **Journey to Jerusalem** *(SM051-060)*, scroll down to **The Grieving Sisters of Bethany – SM052**, and play.

Jonathan Williams

Leave Her Alone!

Men are feasting at a great banquet held for Jesus and his disciples. While they are enjoying the meal, one woman discerns the difficult days ahead and does something to honor Jesus that would be told around the world for all to hear.

Jonathan Williams

10 LEAVE HER ALONE!

It was the last stop before Jerusalem. Jesus and his disciples had traveled many miles from Galilee in the north where his fame was greatest on their final journey to the capital city of God's people, Jerusalem. The disciples did not know it was his last journey. Only Jesus did, and a woman, who gained great insight into the things of God. Her name was Mary and she and her family loved Jesus dearly.

Jesus had been in their home before. We have seen that on his first visit he was teaching the men who were gathered around him while the women busily prepared a meal for their special guest. Well, not all the women were preparing. While Martha was busily engaged in the meal preparations, she noticed her sister was missing and discovered her sitting with the men. And not just sitting with the men – she was up front at Jesus' feet, listening with fascination at every word that came from his mouth, oblivious to all that needed to get done for the meal.

"Lord, don't you care that my sister has left me to do all the work to get this meal ready?" Martha had asked. Jesus replied, "Martha, Martha – you are worried and bothered about so many things when only a few things are necessary, really only one, and Mary has discovered what this one thing is as she sits at my feet."

It was a great lesson for both sisters at this first encounter with Jesus in their home. His compassion for them and the wisdom of his teaching showed the one treasure to be valued above all others – Jesus himself. They believed he was the promised Messiah and their love and devotion to him was steadfast. They knew he had the words of God. They knew he had authority over evil spirits that afflicted men. They knew that in him forgiveness could be found, and they knew that he had power to make the sick well.

When their brother Lazarus fell gravely ill, the sisters urgently and confidently sent their servants to Jesus that he might come and heal him. They knew he would come. Jesus loved them. They knew Jesus loved their brother Lazarus. They knew God would hear their prayer, and Jesus' prayer for healing, and everything would be alright.

But we learned that in their longest night and in their greatest test of faith, Lazarus grew weaker, Jesus did not come, and Lazarus died. The grief was overwhelming. Their beloved brother had unexpectedly died, and their beloved Master, Jesus, had failed them.

So they thought.

He had not come in time to heal Lazarus, and when Jesus did arrive, four days after his death, they wept at his feet, and Jesus wept with them.

But the death of Lazarus was an opportunity to teach the sisters a deeper lesson – Jesus had power to heal, and he had power to raise the dead, and Jesus not only had power to raise the dead but he said, "I am the resurrection and the life, he who believes in me, shall live forever with me."

"Did the sisters believe this?" he asked, and when they said yes Jesus took them to the tomb and raised their brother to life. "Lazarus, come forth," Jesus said, and their dead brother breathed again, walked out of the tomb and lived. Astonishment and indescribable joy swept over the sisters. Their love for Jesus deepened and they were committed to him – the great treasure – above all else.

Not everyone was committed to Jesus. After Jesus raised Lazarus, some of the bystanders, who were not sympathetic to Jesus went to the Pharisees and told them what he had done. The Pharisees went to the chief priests in the Temple in Jerusalem and told them. They convened a council and debated.

"What are we doing? This Jesus is a deceiver and is performing great signs. If we let him go on like this, he will continue to perform such signs and all the people will believe in him."

Another said, "Yes, and this will only stir up the Romans. They always are watchful for insurrection. When they see all the people following Jesus they will take it as a threat, and they will come and remove us from our place of leadership and destroy our nation."

Caiaphas, the high priest, listened for some time as the council discussed the problem of Jesus but didn't seem to know what to do with him. It was clear that he was performing many miracles, but they did not believe the miracles were from God. They believed Jesus was a deceiver, but what should they do about him? Finally, Caiaphas spoke, "Brothers, brothers, please! Quiet!

It is clear from this discussion that none of you knows what to do. But I believe our course of action is clear. One man must die. Either this man dies, or the nation dies. Either we arrest Jesus or we lose our nation to the Romans."

All fell quiet. It was a conclusion many of them had thought about for some time – that Jesus must die – but they had been afraid to say it aloud. Now Caiaphas had uttered the words that the religious leaders had wanted to hear all along – they must do away with Jesus – and from that point on they planned to kill him and gave orders that if anyone found him, they must report his location so they could arrest him.

~~~

The Passover of the Jews was near. Pilgrims from across the land and from the far corners of the Roman empire journeyed to Jerusalem for the festival. As they journeyed and as they congregated in the Temple in preparation for the great feast that commemorated their deliverance from Egypt, many asked, "Do you think Jesus is coming to the feast? And if he comes, what will he do? What will the leaders do for there is a rumor they are sending out word for his arrest." And the people wondered what would take place in the days to come.

Jesus and his disciples were finishing the long walk from Jericho to Jerusalem, 17 long miles upward from the desert floor to the mountains of Judea. But rather than go straight to Jerusalem, Jesus stopped in one of his favorite places. It was the city where Mary, Martha, and Lazarus lived. Jesus was in Bethany. But this time, he was enjoying a meal at the house of Simon the leper, one of the lepers that he had healed.

The disease of leprosy that afflicted many people in that part of the world was doubly difficult. It was difficult because of the obvious physical infirmity that it brought, and it was difficult because it cut off a person from the rest of the community. When Jesus healed the lepers, it was a double healing, for the person's affliction was gone and the person could be restored to the community and enter into the social life of friends, family, and worshippers of God. In coming to the home of Simon the leper, Jesus was showing that Simon was physically healed and restored to the family of God.

Many people were there. The disciples, Mary, Martha, and Lazarus. Martha was busily engaged in the kitchen preparing supper for this great host of people, and the crowds swarmed around the house. Some came into the great banquet room and stood along the walls to watch the feast. They wanted to see Jesus and they wanted to see Lazarus for all knew Lazarus had died, was buried in his tomb for four days, and that Jesus had raised him. But not everyone in this crowd was full of joy. Some were spies from the council of the religious leaders and they were sent to arrest Jesus. They were also sent to kill Lazarus for because of his resurrection the number of people who believed in Jesus grew.

Finally, it was time for the meal and the men came in to recline at the table. First came Simon the leper for he was the host. He welcomed the disciples, then Jesus, and there at Jesus' side was Lazarus, alive and full of health and vitality. Some of the people whispered, "It is true. There is Lazarus! He did raise Lazarus. Praise be to God! Jesus must be the Messiah."

Simon the leper turned to Jesus and said, "Master, restorer of life, will you offer our prayer of thanks before we recline at table." All grew quiet, Jesus lifted his face and his hands to heaven and said,

"Blessed are You, O Lord our God, King of the Universe, who brings forth bread from the earth." All said amen, the servants began to wash the men's feet and anoint them before they reclined at table, the women prepared to serve, the crowd stood along the walls, but someone was missing.

Where was Mary?

She had not been in the kitchen helping her sister, and this time Martha did not seem to be disturbed as she and her helpers joyfully prepared the meal for Jesus and her brother, for Simon and the disciples. Martha half expected to see her bold sister, Mary, in the room with the men, listening to Jesus and preparing to eat with them! But when she looked around the banquet room, Mary was nowhere to be seen.

Where was Mary?

She was mingling with the crowd. She wanted to be close to Jesus, but there was no approaching him. Simon, the disciples, and her brother Lazarus seemed to have Jesus' full attention and Mary did not sense that it was right for her to be among them at this time. Besides, she was happy for her brother, Lazarus, to be close to Jesus and to learn more from him.

Then Mary heard disturbing whispers. "He is here, and Lazarus is here too." And when Mary looked in their direction they quickly stopped talking and turned away as if they did not want her to hear what they were saying. The men looked evil and Mary sensed they were not there to learn but were there to cause harm.

A few minutes later she heard more whispering, "he must die and the other one must die, too." And this time Mary grew alarmed but just when she was about to go to Jesus to tell him these words she heard the voice of Jesus rise up. It was a sad voice and he said,

"I have been with you for these years and I have taught you many things about the kingdom of God. You have seen the power of the kingdom," and Jesus turned to Simon the leper and all knew that Jesus was referring to his healing. "You have seen that the power of the kingdom of God is greater than all sickness, greater than all spirits, greater than all sin, and greater even than death." And Jesus turned to Lazarus and shouts of praise went up for God's great work in raising Lazarus from the dead.

> The power of the kingdom of God is greater than all sickness, greater than all spirits, greater than all sin, and greater even than death.

"But I tell you this and you must understand, the kingdom of God is like a seed that God plants in the ground and there it remains until a day when new life comes and it rises above the ground, but before the seed can give life it must first be buried.

"He who has ears to hear, let him hear."

And then the women began bringing out the first dishes for the men to eat.

Mary stood for a while transfixed by his words. She thought on his words that the kingdom was like a seed that must first be buried before it could rise with new life, and she thought on the evil men in their presence who were there to harm Jesus and her brother if only they had the chance. And then it all came to her at once. "Yes," she thought, "yes," and she left the great feast at Simon's house and hurried to her home to retrieve something special.

She went into her room and located a treasure that she had owned for many years. It was a gift from her father when she became a young woman. She had often thought about using it. But the treasure was so valuable and so precious that she never felt it was the right occasion for its use. It was an alabaster jar filled with perfume. The jar itself was valuable and was taxed heavily when it was imported from the exotic lands of the East. But the contents of the jar were even more precious for it was pure nard – the exotic anointing oil and perfume made from a plant of the Far East. One drop of nard would emit a lovely fragrance and the entire bottle was worth the wages of a man working a full year.

Mary picked up the nard and said, "Yes, this is what I have been saving it for," and she walked back to the house of Simon the Leper, her heart filled with love, devotion, and determination for what she must do.

When she entered, the servants were almost done washing the feet of all the men and anointing them with drops of oil upon their heads as the food was served. They were just about to wash Jesus' feet when Mary gently said, "No, please, stop."

Everyone looked in her direction. Why was this woman giving instruction to a man? Why was this woman in this gathering of men? She was not bringing in a dish of food for the men to eat. Why was she speaking, and why did she not want the servants to wash the feet of Jesus?

Then Mary stepped forward and went to the place where Jesus reclined. She opened her precious alabaster jar and poured some on his head. The men could not believe how much she poured and they gasped. Did she not know how expensive that was? Then she went to Jesus' feet and they could not believe what they were witnessing. Mary poured the rest of the bottle of pure nard upon Jesus' feet, rubbed the oil into his feet, loosened her hair, and began to dry his feet with her long, beautiful hair.

The men were shocked. This was not appropriate behavior for a woman, but Mary did not care for she was honoring her Lord and preparing him for the suffering that lay ahead.

> Mary, dearest Mary, the one who had sat at his feet learning, the one who wept at his feet grieving, was now kneeling at his feet, worshipping.

Jesus watched as Mary, dearest Mary, the one who had sat at his feet learning, the one who wept at his feet grieving, was now kneeling at his feet, worshipping. Jesus' heart filled with joy and love as he saw this daughter of Abraham preparing him for the suffering that was ahead. He was about to reach down and bless her when some of the disciples sprang up and said,

"I'm sorry, but this is enough! It's one thing to anoint Jesus with some of it, and that is proper and good, but you could have sold the rest of this perfume for a high price and given the money to the poor."

Judas Iscariot, one of the twelve, stood up and said, "Brothers, you are right. If she had given the jar to me I would have sold it for the wages of an entire year. Think of how much money that would have been. Think of how many poor people we could have helped." And as Judas said these words he moved toward Mary and grabbed her arm, and then Jesus said,

"No, you stop, all of you. You do not understand. Leave her alone!

Go back to your place Judas! All of you men, go back to your couches and eat. She has done a good deed to me. You always have the poor with you. Anytime you wish you can go to the poor and give them something, but you will not always have me."

Jesus looked around at his men who were ashamed and confused. Then Jesus said to them, "Did you not hear what I said about the kingdom being like a seed that is buried? She has heard and understood, and when she poured this perfume on my body she did it to prepare me for my burial."

Jesus reached down toward Mary and she looked up from his feet. Tears were in her eyes as she heard Jesus speak of his death and burial. Though she did not fully understand, she more than anyone else knew that dark days lay ahead for him. Then Jesus said, "Truly I say to all of you, the gospel of the kingdom of God will be preached in the whole world to all the nations and when it is, what Mary has done for me will be told to all."

Mary got up and with joy in her heart walked to her sister Martha who embraced her with love and said, "You have done a great thing, sister! Shall we now serve them the rest of the food before it gets cold?" And with a smile on her face, Mary followed Martha into the kitchen where they picked up the heavy dishes full of good food and together they gladly served Jesus, his disciples, Simon the leper, and their brother Lazarus.

The men ate in silence, but the perfume lingered long in the air and the words of Jesus about his burial stirred the hearts of all who wondered why he had said such a thing and what it meant.

The next day, Jesus and his disciples awakened. Jesus looked upon his men. There was Peter, James, John, and Andrew, huddling and talking quietly. There was Philip who had followed him from his earliest days of ministry and Bartholomew, Matthew the tax collector, Thomas, James the son of Alphaeus, Thaddaeus, and Simon the zealot.

Then, with an ominous sound in his voice Jesus asked, "Where is Judas?" And one of the disciples said, "Lord, we do not know. As we were sleeping we could hear him groaning and muttering to himself. He was saying harsh words as if he were very angry. And then, he got up in the middle of the night."

Just at that moment Judas walked back into the room and Peter said, "Judas, we were just talking about you. Where have you been?"

"None of your business," Judas said and then he looked at Jesus and their eyes locked. "I ... I ... you just don't need to know, Peter." And then Judas looked away for he knew that Jesus knew where he had gone during the night and that he had met with those who were plotting to kill him and that Judas had said,

I will betray him to you, soon, during one of these nights, when he is away from the crowds I will lead you to him. What will you give me for this?" When they counted out 30 pieces of silver he said, "This is not enough. This is the price to pay for a slave."

"Exactly," they said "for that is what we think of your Jesus. He is no better than a lowly slave and if you don't cooperate with us, you will see what we will do to you."

"Alright, alright," said Judas, "just wait and I will lead you to him in secret."

The conversation was playing in the mind of Judas and it seemed that Jesus could see it all and hear it all. Jesus looked upon Judas as if he were looking upon a venomous snake and then he said, "The time has now come. Today, we are going to Jerusalem."

~~~

This story marks the beginning of Jesus' final week that would be the darkest and most glorious week in human history for in it Jesus did his greatest work and opened the door to eternal life. He died for the sins of mankind and three days later rose from the dead as Lord of all. When the women went to the tomb to anoint his body with oils and spices, they were too late for he had risen.

But one woman was not too late! Because of Mary's heart of worship, she experienced what no one else experienced – she anointed his body for his greatest work!

Mary is an example to us. She gave her most precious treasure and spent it all on Jesus. What have we given to him? What is our most valued possession? Our greatest treasure is our heart. We have the opportunity to break it open and pour our love upon Jesus for all he has done for us. When we do this, some may protest. Some may say, "Why are you doing this? Why are you lavishing all this upon Jesus? Why are you wasting your life upon him?" But we must not fear or listen to their protests.

Pour out your heart, pour out your love to him!

Read the Story as Originally Told in John 11:47-12:11

7:47 Therefore the chief priests and the Pharisees convened a council, and were saying, "What are we doing? For this man is performing many signs. 48 If we let Him go on like this, all men will believe in Him, and the Romans will come and take away both our place and our nation." [49] But one of them, Caiaphas, who was high priest that year, said to them, "You know nothing at all, [50] nor do you take into account that it is expedient for you that one man die for the people, and that the whole nation not perish." [51] Now he did not say this on his own initiative, but being high priest that year, he prophesied that Jesus was going to die for the nation, [52] and not for the nation only, but in order that He might also gather together into one the children of God who are scattered abroad. [53] So from that day on they planned together to kill Him.

[54] Therefore Jesus no longer continued to walk publicly among the Jews, but went away from there to the country near the wilderness, into a city called Ephraim; and there He stayed with the disciples.

[55] Now the Passover of the Jews was near, and many went up to Jerusalem out of the country before the Passover to purify themselves. [56] So they were seeking for Jesus, and were saying to one another as they stood in the temple, "What do you think; that He will not come to the feast at all?" [57] Now the chief priests and the Pharisees had given orders that if anyone knew where He was, he was to report it, so that they might seize Him.

[12:1] Jesus, therefore, six days before the Passover, came to Bethany where Lazarus was, whom Jesus had raised from the dead. [2] So they made Him a supper there, and Martha was serving; but Lazarus was one of those reclining at the table with Him. [3] Mary then took a pound of very costly perfume of pure nard, and anointed the feet of Jesus and wiped His feet with her hair; and the house was filled with the fragrance of the perfume. [4] But Judas Iscariot, one of His disciples, who was intending to betray Him, said, [5] "Why was this perfume not sold for three hundred denarii

and given to poor people?" *6* Now he said this, not because he was concerned about the poor, but because he was a thief, and as he had the money box, he used to pilfer what was put into it. *7* Therefore Jesus said, "Let her alone, so that she may keep it for the day of My burial. *8* For you always have the poor with you, but you do not always have Me."

9 The large crowd of the Jews then learned that He was there; and they came, not for Jesus' sake only, but that they might also see Lazarus, whom He raised from the dead. *10* But the chief priests planned to put Lazarus to death also; *11* because on account of him many of the Jews were going away and were believing in Jesus.

Cultural and Historical Insights

➤ A meal such as this was held in two stages. In the first stage initial courses were served, and it was also a time for servants to wash the hands and feet of guests and anoint them with perfumes. In stage two, the main courses would be offered.

➤ For a woman to be present at a meal would be highly unusual and she would usually be considered a woman with questionable reputation.

➤ A perfume worth such a large sum would never be lavished upon one person and some of the value would be sold and given to the poor.

➤ Alabaster jars were five to nine inches long and made out of ground translucent calcite stone. They were imported from India and the Far East and were heavily taxed. Thus, they were worth considerable sums to the purchasers.

These insights are from *A Social Science Commentary on the*

Synoptic Gospels by Bruce Malina, Fortress Press, 128.

Reflection

Why do you think the Pharisees and others did not believe in Jesus even though he had raised Lazarus from the dead? Does this say anything about human nature and a hardness of heart to believe?

_____

_____

_____

Why do you think Jesus chose to eat his meal in Bethany in the home of Simon the Leper? What would this say to the whole community in Bethany about Jesus eating with a man who had been an outcast?

_____

_____

_____

How would you describe Mary's heart toward Jesus? Would you say you have this kind of heart toward him?

_____

_____

_____

The account in John tells us that Judas was upset with Mary because he was greedy and wanted the nard for himself. The accounts in Matthew (26:6-13) and Mark (14:3-9) show us that other disciples were upset with Mary's action. Why do you think they were upset?

_____

_____

_____

Jesus said, "The poor you have with you always, but you do not always have me." Why did Jesus say this, what did he mean, and how can we apply this in our relationship to Jesus?

_____

_____

_____

Listen to this story online at http://wgsministries.org/stories/ministry/. Click on The **Journey to Jerusalem** *(SM051-060)*, scroll down to **Leave Her Alone – SM060**, and play.

The Greater Story

The events in Jesus' life and the stories he told are among the greatest stories the world has heard. You have read ten of them in this book and you can read many others, learn more about his life, and discover the purpose for which he came in the Gospels of Matthew, Mark, Luke, and John.

Storytelling captures imaginations and hearts. Undoubtedly, this is why Jesus was such a great storyteller. But he designed his stories to draw attention to a Greater Story – the Story he lived. In this Greater Story he and his audience were participants. So are you! So am I! What is the Greater Story in which we play a role? Like a good play, it consists of several Acts.

Act 1 – Creation
Act 2 – Catastrophe
Act 3 – Covenants
Act 4 – Christ
Act 5 – Commission
Act 6 – Consummation

Act 1 – Creation tells about the Creator. He is the all powerful God. He is One. No other God exists. He makes all things to express His majesty and beauty including humanity. Humanity is the pinnacle of His creation. God made man and woman in his image to reflect his character. They are to be creative in their fulfilling of the amazing destiny he gives them – to manage and rule the earth for His glory and for the good of all mankind.[6]

---

[6] Read about this in Genesis 1-2.

Act 2 – Catastrophe introduces sadness into the Story. Something goes terribly wrong in Paradise. The man and woman turn away from the Creator. In an unthinkable act, they rebel against God and seek to establish their own authority. They introduce sin into the world, and its consequences – suffering, sorrow, and death – follow close behind. As they bear children and their children multiply throughout the earth, the consequences of the rebellion cannot be shaken off and spread to all mankind.[7]

Act 3 – Covenants introduces a new figure in the drama. His name is Abraham. The Creator makes a covenant with him and promises blessings climaxing in the greatest blessing of all – through his descendants One will come who will rescue humanity from its rebellion and death. The descendants of Abraham become the nation, Israel. Israel is a light in the dark world. It exists to point the nations to the true God – the Creator of the universe. But Israel fails in its mission. It becomes like the other rebellious nations of the world and must be judged. Israel's prophets tell of a Coming One who will restore the nation to its purpose and bring restoration to all mankind. He will bring salvation to the ends of the earth.[8]

Act 4 – Christ is the turning point in the Story. The Promised One comes! His name is Jesus. He takes the Story to a new and dramatic level. He lives among his people with humility and grace. He heals the sick, gives sight to the blind, and raises the dead. He sets free the oppressed, forgives sin, and tells stories of God's great love. Not everyone is happy with his mission. The political

---

[7] Read about this in Genesis 3-11.

[8] Read about **the covenant with Abraham** in Genesis 12 and 15. You can find his entire story in Genesis 12-25. Read about **the covenant with Israel** in Exodus 19-20. You can read Israel's story in the Old Testament, Exodus through Malachi.

authorities are threatened. The religious authorities are suspicious and finally cannot condone his mission because it does not match their ideas of what the Deliverer will do. They conspire to arrest and try him. They crucify Him for the crimes of blasphemy and revolution. Three days later, he rises from the dead, gathers His followers, and prepares them for Act 5.[9]

Act 5 – Commission is when the resurrected Jesus commands his followers to go into the world and tell everyone the good news. The promise that God made to Abraham that he would bless the entire world will now come to pass because the Promised One has come. He lived among us. He died for our sins. He rose from the dead and is enthroned as the Lord of all. He gives his Spirit to empower his people to spread the joyful news that God will forgive all our sins. God and humanity can be reconciled. The original destiny God gave mankind, to display his image and to rule the world for his glory, can now be restored.[10]

This good news has now come as far as you! What will you do with it? The most famous verse in the Bible, John 3:16 says:

> For God so loved the world that He gave His only begotten Son, that whoever believes in Him shall not perish but have eternal life.

Act 6 – Consummation Jesus will return and judge the world. Every person will give an account for his life. Every knee will bow and confess that Jesus is Lord of all and the only Savior of the

---

[9] Read about Jesus in the Gospels of the New Testament – Matthew, Mark, Luke, and John.
[10] You can find the Great Commission in these verses: Matthew 28:18-20; Mark 16:15-16; Luke 24:44-49; John 20:21; and Acts 1:8. You can read about the first efforts to proclaim the good news in the world in the Book of Acts.

world. Those who receive him will enter into eternal life. Those who do not will be separated from his love.[11]

God wants you to receive his love and to be part of the Greater Story. He also wants you to bring the good news to others. Who do you know that needs to hear his Story? Why not pass this book to your friends. Pray for them and help them find God's abundant love and help them take their place in the Greater Story.

Yes, Jesus was a great storyteller. He told stories that captured the imaginations of His listeners. But he told the stories so that those who heard could take on significant roles in the unfolding of the great drama of history. Are you ready to take your part in the Greater Story?

We would like to hear from you and encourage you. If you have received Christ as your Savior or if you have taken a significant step to forgive others or to release yourself from self-imposed captivity, would you write us and tell us your story?

You can write us at:

Word of God, Speak
PO Box 90047
San Antonio, TX 78209

You can also reach on the web at www.WGSministries.org. We look forward to hearing from you!

---

[11] You can read a quick overview of the end in 1 Corinthians 15:20-28 and Revelation 20-22.

ABOUT THE AUTHOR, JONATHAN WILLIAMS

Jonathan pastored for over 35 years and is now the president of Word of God, Speak – a teaching ministry that advances life change, builds a biblical worldview, and connects people to God's story of love for the world.

He is the Bible teacher for the daily program, *The Heaven & Home Hour* and the creator of and storyteller for *Stories of the Master*, a weekly radio broadcast heard around the world. *Stories of the Master* retells the story of Jesus and the stories he told bringing in historical and cultural details which we modern people often miss, but details which make the stories come alive.

Jonathan was married to his first wife, Dee for 27 years. She is now with the Lord. They had three children and now have five grandchildren. Jonathan now lives in San Antonio, Texas with his wife Kathleen, his co-worker and best friend.

For more information about Jonathan's ministry, contact him at
WGS ♦ PO Box 90047 ♦ San Antonio, TX 78209.
Email: jonathan@WGSpeak.org
www.WGSministries.org
1.800.248.4687

Other books by Jonathan Williams

The Prodigal Son and His Prodigal Father
Dead Men Rising: The Death of Sin/The Rise of Grace in Romans 6:1-14
Dead Men Rising Study Guide
Resurrection Vision
Grace for Every Day

ABOUT THE ARTIST, SCOTT FREEMAN

The cover illustration for *The Women Jesus Loved* is an original oil painting by Scott Freeman. Scott is a Fine Artist, art theatre performer, and award-winning children's book author and illustrator. Scott earned his BFA in Painting from the Kansas City Art Institute in 1982, where he also met his artist wife, Mollie. They have five children. Jonathan Williams was Scott's pastor for several years in Kansas City.

After working as an artist/designer for Hallmark Cards in Kansas City for nearly 10 years, Scott moved his family to Loveland, Colorado in 2001 so that he and Mollie could pursue their fine art careers full time. Scott loves to express his faith through his art and he frequently speaks and paints in churches and at other events. He also teaches art classes and competes in open-air painting festivals around the country. His award-winning work is now collected throughout the U.S. and overseas.

You can view Scott and Mollie's work at their shared website: www.freemanartgallery.com.

ABOUT STORIES OF THE MASTER

Stories of the Master is Jonathan Williams weekly storytelling program. He incorporates historical and cultural details from the works of scholars such as Dr. Kenneth Bailey and Gary Burge. Dr. Bailey spent 40 years living and teaching New Testament in Egypt, Lebanon, Jerusalem, and Cyprus. He is the emeritus research professor of Middle Eastern New Testament studies for the Tantur Ecumenical Institute in Jerusalem and is the author of many enlightening works including *Jesus Through Middle Eastern Eyes*. Dr. Gary Burge Is professor of New Testament at Wheaton College and the author of numerous books including *Jesus: The Middle Eastern Storyteller*.

Stories of the Master is heard worldwide on Spirit Network Radio and on many other stations. You can hear all the stories online at www.WGSministries.org/Stories. The goal of this storytelling program is to introduce people to Jesus of Nazareth. The events in his life and the stories he told are among the most famous worldwide. It is our belief and hope that as people hear of Jesus, his power over sickness, evil spirits, sin, and death, they will be attracted to him and want to learn more about his mission to establish the kingdom of God and his vision for the world.

You can bring Jonathan to your church to hear these stories live. People have always loved stories. It's time for the world to hear again, *The Stories of the Master*! Contact him at PO Box 90047 ♦ San Antonio, TX 78209.

Jonathan Williams